# BAST

# BAST

## Dark Genesis

### LATOY P. HOUSTON

#### Illustrator: Latavya Latson

**LYNX** PUBLISHERS

This book is a work of fiction. Names, characters, businesses, organizations, places, events and incidents either are the product of the author's imagination or are used fictitiously. Any resemblance to actual persons, living or dead, events, or locales is entirely coincidental.

Published in the United States of America by Lynx Publishers.

## Mystery/ Crime Fiction

### Trigger Warnings:

- Rape/ Sexual Assault
- Drugs
- Child abuse/ pedophilia
- Incest
- Kidnapping
- Death
- Blood
- Mental illness
- Self-injurious behavior

A STORY ABOUT A SOCIAL WORKER WHO SOLVES CASES ONE PUNCH AT A TIME.

# DEDICATION

This book is dedicated to all victims who have suffered from childhood trauma.

Never forget that YOU are worthy of love!

God, therapy, and self-love are the keys to stopping a potential generational curse.

Do not give up on yourself,

Be your own superhero!

**You got this!**

People who inspired me to keep writing: My mother, Joyce Latson, Uncle Tony, Andrew, and an entire entourage of family and friends that's always there for me.

I want to also give a huge shout out to my children: Jordan, Arianna, Brandon, Trinitee, and Nathan. Thank you for supporting me!

Follow me:

 @Bast_DarkGenesis

Email: bast.darkgenesis1@gmail.com

# TABLE OF CONTENTS

# INTRODUCTION

Sometimes I sit and speculate on how my life would have been if my past were different. Would I still be the person I am now? I realize everybody goes through tough times, and I recognize that there are people who have a past that is much worse than mine, and they turned out all right. Not me. My life did not turn out so great. I am disturbed and bitter because I suffered as a child; Therefore, people must pay. Not just the monsters that hurt me, but others just like them. They will pay for what they did to me, and they will pay for what they are doing to others. I demand vengeance; however, my vengeance is different; I am in a battle with myself when choosing to do good or to do evil. It should be easy, but it is not! By day, I am Journey Anders, a social worker with Child Protective Services in Dallas, Texas.

My duties are to care for children who are being victimized and ignored. At first glance, you would notice that my appearance and manner are always professional, and I always wear business attire. I try to keep my natural hair tamed, but I change my hairstyle from time to time…it is easier to just pick my fro and go! By night, I am a different person; my masked and tight-fitted attire is for one purpose only: to fight. They call me "Bast". I get rid of people who have harmed children after the justice system had failed them when they needed help the most. If I do not get my way during the day, I most definitely will get my way at night!

# Chapter One

And the God of all grace, who called you to
his eternal glory in Christ, after you have
suffered a little while, will himself restore you
and make you strong, firm, and steadfast.
1 Peter 5:10

*Green:* *represents growth and renewal, the*
*color of rebirth*

# BAST: Dark Genesis

You know how you can sometimes forget what you cooked last week, what you wore three days ago, or what you watched on TV last night? Well, your brain remembers what it wants to remember, like that amazing chicken alfredo I made two days ago. However, sometimes my brain remembers what I wish it would forget... like that chicken I tried to fry that ended up like a weird science experiment in my kitchen.

When I was six years old, something very traumatic happened to me. I tried so many times to erase it from my memory, but at twenty-four, I still remember it, just like it happened to me yesterday. It was a cold night; I was walking alone, and every animal outside that you could think of was chasing, attacking, biting, and scratching me. There were owls, wolves, bears, and many more. I was screaming at the top of my lungs, but nobody heard me, nobody saved me, nobody cared. I was in so much pain, so much unbearable pain, and eventually, I died.

Dramatic, right? That really did not happen, but that over-the-top and exaggerated story is how my real story felt. Truth is... I wish that had happened to me because my reality hurts more. The real story is that after my mom and dad divorced many years ago, my mom started dating this guy named Al. He gave her roses every weekend, but soon after she fell in love with him, he moved in, and the roses stopped coming. Eventually, she found out he was an alcoholic, and there was a rumor going around that he was doing drugs, but Mom never believed the gossip. No matter what, my mom forgave him, and she stuck by his side.

As she got to know Al, Mom understood he was battling with something, but he never wanted to talk about it. One night, she woke up out of her sleep around three in the morning and found Al standing on the bed, on top of the headboard. He was asleep and talking to himself while keeping his balance on the headboard. Mom was able to get him down and back in bed, then prayed over him until she fell asleep. In those days, my mom was at the beginning stage of her religious journey. There were many nights like that, but the one that scared me the most was the night Mom said Al started screaming in the middle of the night, pointing at a corner in the bedroom. She had a hard time calming him down.

"It's right there!! It won't leave me alone!" He yelled.

Mom told me she jumped out of bed and turned on the light, and kept telling him she did not see anything.

He was so terrified that he started crying and whispered, "It left the room. It went inside Journey's room!"

Mom ran to my room and found me asleep. She assured Al there was nothing in the house, but she knew something was going on with him. Some nights, he would throw punches in the air while he was asleep. All Mom would do is pray for him. It is crazy because he never remembered what happened at night, and he never remembered his dreams, so Mom never talks to him about his night.

One night before Mom left for work, she had a huge fight with Al and told him that if he did not stop drinking, she would leave him. Al shrugged his shoulders and angrily shouted, "You're all talk, woman. You need me!"

Mom never stood up for herself. I needed her to that night. I am not sure she knew that it was the other way around. Al needed her. If she ever kicked him out of her house, he would have been alone and homeless. Nevertheless, no matter how obvious everything was, my mom was completely blinded by love. I hated that her hours switched to night, but that shift paid more, and Al was fired from his job again because of his drinking. She needed the extra money to keep up with the bills. That night, Mom thought it would be okay to leave me with Al since three of my cousins were there, but my cousins only came over to get drunk and high with Al. They were all high school dropouts and not doing anything important with their lives. Every time they came over, my cousins always bullied me and ordered me around, so I was never excited to see them.

When Mom left that night, Al was already drunk and kept stumbling over everything all night. I do not know how many drinks he had, but it was a lot. I remember being hungry and going to Al. I was hoping he would buy me a burger and fries from somewhere. I knocked on his bedroom door. When he did not answer, I opened it. He was sitting at the foot of the bed with my cousins, looking down with their backs toward me. After Al noticed me in his room, he started moving quickly and then slid something underneath his bed. I did not know it then, but it was drugs. He yelled at me for being in his room. When I did not respond to his anger, Al slapped me, then pushed me onto the bed. My cousins stood up and started laughing at me. By that time, I was overwhelmed with anger and kicked one of my cousins who was closest to me. He balled his fist and plunged for me; Al stopped him before he touched me, but then he unzipped his pants.

"Take your pants off!" Al demanded.

I was extremely confused by what was happening. When I refused, my cousins ran over to me and held me down. It was like everything was planned. Al took my pants off and raped me. My cousins watched, then took turns raping me. I fought and screamed, but nothing seemed to work. Not even the sight of blood oozing from my body was enough to make them stop. This went on until I turned nine, and happened every night my mother left for work. She was a registered nurse and worked long hours overnight. He and my cousins took my childhood and innocence from me, and the molestation only stopped after I told my father. I would spend the night at my father's house every other weekend, but I always kept that deep, dark secret about Al and my cousins to myself because Al threatened to beat Mom if I told my secret to anyone.

# BAST: Dark Genesis

The night I told my father my secret, he did not suspect anything was wrong. He was just checking up on me. My father and I had a close relationship. If I had to choose, I would have chosen my father to be my custodial parent; our bond was very tight. However, Dad keeping me all the time would not work; he was always fighting someone! He never stayed at a job longer than six months; he just did not like putting up with things or people that didn't make sense to him, and he definitely didn't put up with any disrespect! That is why it was hard for me to tell him my secret, but I knew it was time for me to talk.

I was in his living room, sitting down, when my father called me into his bathroom with him. He was getting ready to take me out on our father-daughter date. He always takes me to the movies to see any movie I want. I always looked forward to doing this every weekend. When I walked into the bathroom, he was in the middle of brushing his teeth.

"Journey!" He roared passionately while splashing toothpaste everywhere.

"Do you know why we named you Journey?" he asked.

"Daddy! You tell me this story all the time. Yes! I know why, it's because I am your reason why." I said conceitedly.

I was acting annoyed, but I secretly like saying that.

"That's right, baby girl. You are the reason why I am no longer a little boy! It was a *journey* turning this hardheaded teenage boy into the man that I am today! he said proudly while hitting himself on his chest.

"You're so corny, Dad, and can you please finish brushing your teeth?" I said, laughing.

"Ha-ha baby girl, is there anything you want to tell me?" He asked.

I was shocked, scared, and confused. Is he talking about what I think he is talking about? How did he know? Did he know? Many thoughts ran through my mind. He sat me down on his toilet while he had his back turned to me, brushing his teeth. He looked up in the mirror at me and repeated himself.

"Baby girl, why are you quiet? Is there anything you would like to tell me? I am asking because your mother tells me you are acting differently at home, and you are barely talking to her. What is up? You can tell me!"

As he started brushing his teeth again, I knew now was the time to talk about it, and I did not want to lie to him. I took a deep breath, and I told him. I told him everything. The look that he had on his face was every emotion at one time. His eyes were huge. I know he was not expecting the response that I gave him, and he was probably expecting me to say that I had a crush on someone. I told him something that no parent would want to hear about their child. When I finished talking, he hugged me tightly for a long time and cried. I have never seen my dad cry before. What happened after that is very blurry to me. Everything happened so quickly! All I know is that four people are dead now, and I will never see my father outside of prison again. Even though his actions were not how I would have handled it, he is still my dad, and for that reason, he will always be my hero, never forgetting what he has done for me.

After everything happened, my mother felt guilty for what Al and my cousins did to me, but I used to always tell her not to feel that way because it was not her fault. I would have my moments also when I thought about my dad. I missed him so much! In middle school, there were times when kids teased me because I never spoke to anyone and was shy. In time, I became fed up. I had had enough of people constantly picking on me. It reminded me of all the bullying I had endured with my cousins. I walked home, grabbed a knife from the kitchen, went into my bedroom, and just cried for what seemed like hours. I stared at the knife, trying to figure out what I would do with it, called myself awful names, and even scratched my face as I stared in the mirror, I finally grabbed the knife, thinking *I can do it*, thinking everything will be better if I just did it, and when I finally thought I had built enough courage to slice my wrist, my mother walked in, snatched the knife from my hand, threw it on the ground and just hugged me like she never hugged me before. Without saying a word, we both just cried.

The next day was Saturday. She told me to get in the car and would not tell me where we were going. All she did was stare at me with her tearful eyes and say, "I failed you once, I won't fail you again!" We pulled up to what looked like a huge empty warehouse, but there was only one car outside. A man, who had on what looked like a karate gi, was standing outside as if he were waiting for us.

"Thu! Hello, are we late?" Mom was waving uncontrollably as if she had just seen a relative she had not seen in years.

"Oh no, Ms. Hollis. You are right on time… So, this must be Journey. Hello, I have heard so much about you. I am Thu Le, your trainer."

As he extended his hand for a shake, I looked at Mom; she was motioning for me to shake his hand. I glanced at his hand and then stepped back. "Wait. Trainer? Why?"

"Journey, I have heard so much about you. I know this may seem a little weird and maybe confusing, but I want to earn your trust. I work with your mother at the hospital. The love that your mother has for you, I only imagine my mom loving me the same way. I never experienced her love as an adult because they took her from me when I was a kid. Please, allow me to show you that every darkness ends with light."

As I stood there, lost, he explained that the importance of perseverance and excellence comes from martial arts and that this is the way of life. This was also a way to get a sense of justice and respect, and it's not about learning how to fight to beat people up, but more about gaining clarity and purpose for my life, and would also assist me mentally and will have many physical benefits.

For some strange reason, I trusted everything he was telling me. The way he looked into my eyes as he spoke forced me to listen to every word that came out of his mouth. That was day one of many days to come where I not only learned different martial arts, but Thu became someone I respected and loved. He gave me advice, counseled me, and was my friend. There were days when I wanted to give up, many days where I cried, and many days I came home with bruises and some minor broken bones from days I was being too stubborn to rest. But when I came home complaining to my mother about my training, all she would do was say, "Train for your father." That would be all that I needed to get me motivated again, and I would train for hours, train every single day as if my life depended on it. Except on Sundays…Mama made sure I gave that day to the Lord and attended church, even sang in the choir sometimes, but as soon as Monday came, I was back on my mission.

By the time I made it to high school, my physique had changed a lot. I was getting a lot of attention from boys and girls. I was muscular, but very feminine. My curvy body was a huge distraction and had made me a little cocky, and my attitude was worse. I did not put up with any crap, yet people wanted to test me. Many days, I would ignore it because Thu always told me to be slow to anger. I would have to develop a thick skin and ignore what people do and say, but it was hard on some days.

One day, it was all Crystal Johnson's fault. I embarrassed her, but she made me do it. She was the popular girl in school who all the boys wanted to be with. She never liked me, but I always thought she was just secretly jealous of me. In the gym, we were playing volleyball, and Crystal was on the opposite team. My team only needed one more point to win. Crystal and I seemed to go head-to-head as if there were no other players out there. Then my opportunity came. I saw the ball coming my way. It was my time to attack. Everything was riding on my next move. I exerted every bit of energy into my last shot. As I thrust myself into the air with the perfect counter strike, I spiked the ball back towards our opponent's side. Everybody in the gym erupted in applause and a standing ovation with that winning action. I saw the anger on Crystal's face. It was her fault her team lost because she missed the ball, but I did not care that she was upset. The smirk I had on my face was priceless.

The uproar in the gym for our victory followed us into the shower room. I was so happy, and I felt like I was coming out of my shell of being the quiet, timid girl. It lost me in thought as I kept thinking of the look that Crystal had on her face after that ball flew past her. I started laughing to myself while I was undressing by my locker. Suddenly, a chill went down my spine. Someone was running towards me at an alarming speed. It was Crystal trying to hit me. I blocked her hand in mid-swing, then pushed her aggressively to the ground. When she fell, she hit her nose on a table, causing it to bleed. I laughed, then smacked her on the butt and said,

"You're cute and all, but you are not my type."

All I could hear was snickering from the other girls as I exited the locker room. I could have done more damage to her, but I had to show restraint because it could lead to a bigger problem than a simple high school rivalry. No one knew about all the training I was doing. If they did, they would not try to test me. After I let everyone see a taste of what I could do, Crystal never bothered me again, but I did catch her boyfriend sending me flirtatious vibes from time to time. It was funny, but it did not matter much because I was only interested in what happened after school, not during. I never knew why I was training so hard; I just knew I had to do it and, one day, it would all make sense to me. As for college, a situation happened once that I won't ever forget; a perp was sent to jail because of me. I believe that situation truly motivated me even more to graduate with high honors and work for an agency that protects women and children from abuse and neglect. It has been four years since that incident happened, and the victim still sends me Christmas cards thanking me.

Dad was still in prison, but we wrote to each other often, and I tried to see him at least once a month since they moved him three hours away. Mom is a great inspiration in my life, and Thu is always there for me. I was still training with him, but as I got older, training was getting more intense. He is very professional with everything that he does and very stern when giving instructions. He gave out demands and expected me to do everything he said…exactly how he said it, and if I did not or if I messed up, I had to start all over from the beginning. I loved him, though. He was a sweetheart when we were not training. I noticed he had been coming around more, helping Mom with random things around the house ever since I moved out. It was starting to get a little weird with them when I came around because they laughed at the most random things. Like now, I just walked into Mom's house, and as usual, they are laughing!

"What's so funny?" I asked as I opened the front door.

As expected, they did not answer me and awkwardly changed the subject.

"Hey, hero!" Thu stood up and walked towards the door to greet me.

"Hero? Thuuuu… you know how much I don't like that!" I explained as I gave him a three-second gaze.

15

"My day has been fine. But for real, what is up with you and my mom? Do you have a thing for her?" I questioned.

While laughing, Thu asked, "You know why I call you a hero? If it were not for you in college, that poor girl would have been in a far worse predicament if you hadn't stopped—"

Interrupting while rudely clearing my throat, "People like that shouldn't even exist! I wish I could stop every pervert in this world!"

"So, what's stopping you?" Thu had a serious look on his face while staring directly into my eyes.

"What do you mean? I cannot stop every creep from hurting innocent people! I mean, I did just start working for social services, so hopefully, I can help more in that area, but I cannot just go around beating people up for hurting others! *Although that would be impressive if I could!*" I felt so powerful and confident making my point to Thu.

Thu was looking like he was about to karate chop my ego.

"But did it feel good to beat that guy up after you caught him raping that girl in college?" He asked.

"Of course, it did!" I started pacing back and forth. "Thu, that night, I felt like I was at the right place at the right time. I was just trying to clear my head from writing my thesis and decided to take a walk. I started hearing screaming in the distance, ran to it, and found that creep on top of her."

Thu softly grabbed my hands and looked at me sternly; "It took three people to pull you off that guy. They had to send him to the hospital before they sent him to jail. It's because of you that she's still alive…"

Breaking free from Thu's grip. I shouted, "I-I will never forget that day! I felt so powerful that night, I know I could save someone again if I needed to."

"How about both of y'all stop talking about that night, it always makes you so emotional. You were protected that night, baby girl. Never forget what it says in the good book: The Lord is my strength and my shield; my heart trusts in him, and he helps me. My heart leaps for joy, and with my song I praise him. That is from Psalm 28:7. God was protecting you! He was with you and guided you to protect that girl that night, you should give Him praise!" Mom shouted as she praise danced in the kitchen.

Before I could say anything else, Mom interrupted our conversation again as she placed a hot apple pie on the table that she had just got out of the oven.

"I only stopped dancing because I could not find my favorite tambourine!"

Thu and I just stared at each other; I could see in his eyes that he was not done with this conversation.

"Mom, the aroma of this pie reminds me of all my happy childhood memories combined in one room. I'm ready to go back in time!" I said while wrapping my arms around her.

"Girl, stop hugging me so tight! You're bringing my blood pressure up!" She giggled. "And don't be rude, let Thu get his slice first!"

I gave Mom and Thu the evil eye. "I don't know what's going on here, but I will get to the bottom of this! By the way, Thu, do not think I did not notice you changing the subject on me again!"

I did not know if I was reading the wrong signals or not, but if they did have a thing for each other, that would not be a bad thing. I just thought it was funny that they thought they had to hide it from me. It was cute. On another note, it had been five minutes—why were they still carrying on with that awkward laughter?

# Chapter Two

Be strong and courageous. Do not be afraid or terrified because of them, for the Lord your God goes with you; he will never leave you nor forsake you. Deuteronomy 31:6

***Purple:*** *represents power, bravery, wisdom, and ambition*

# BAST: Dark Genesis

Some days were perfect, and other days I wish I could erase them from my memory. I have been working for Child Protective Services (CPS) for five years now. The people I worked with were amazing, and I just loved my job, but it was not always easy. I had different duties with children who were taken out of their homes because of abuse or neglect. Some cases did not always go as I would have liked them to. In fact, I will always remember the case with Cindy Adams. She was only five when she had to be taken out of her home because her dad beat her daily. However, the father did everything right, including completing anger management classes and going to therapy. He fooled everyone, including a judge. They thought he had changed, so they allowed Cindy to go back home. Three days later, police identified a floating body in a lake as Cindy Adams. Her father admitted to beating her to death because she wet her bed, then dumped her body in a lake.

Anger poured through me when the outcome of that case was presented to me. That case made me extremely angry and sad because there was nothing more that I could have done to keep her from going back to his home, but it was completely out of my hands. I was determined not to allow this to happen again and to do whatever it took to keep these kids safe.

Sam and Samantha were brother and sister, aged nine and ten. Their case was brought to me this week. Inside their folder, it says they were living with their mother and their uncle. Sam told a neighborhood friend that Uncle Reece would not stop hurting them and kept making them do nasty things. Their mom says her kids told a lie because they were angry at their uncle. The neighbor's parents called CPS immediately after their child told them what Sam said. The mother would not give consent to have the children examined for sexual abuse because she was certain nothing had happened. When this happens, I go to a judge to get results.

The phone rang.

"Journey Anders, speaking," I answered.

"Hello, Ms. Anders, this is Judge Davis. I have the paperwork ready and signed for... um, let me see. Oh! Here it is, right in front of me: for case number: 4562278."

"Ok, wow! Thank you! That is for Sam and Samantha. That was quick!" I exclaimed.

"Yeah, I wanted you to get these babies out of that house before the weekend and get'em checked out. You should receive it any minute now via fax."

"Yup, just got it! Thanks again. I'm headed to their house right now!"

"Yup, yup. No problem, hero." He hung up.

Hero? Thu still calls me that. I wish I were a genuine hero to these kids. Hopefully, everything will work out in their favor.

When I arrived at the house and rang the doorbell, Mr. Reece answered the door. He seemed shocked to see me after reading my badge.

"Hello, Reece Whitman? I am here from Child Protective Services to take the children in for questioning and perform other services. I have a court order if you'd like to see it."

Angrily, he shouted, "Questioning? No, I will not allow it!"

"Sir, I have to advise you that if you do not allow me to take the children, I will have to contact the authorities," I responded calmly.

He looked like he was about to do something stupid, so I began positioning myself for anything crazy he had in mind. I was eager to let this tiger out of her cage. *C'mon, Reece, baby, just give me a reason to put my fist down your throat!*

"Um… hold on, what was your name again?" He asked while sweating and turning red in the face.

"Ms. Anders." I held the badge close to his face.

"Ok, Ms. Anders, I will get them ready now. Hold on a minute." He spoke.

Dang! I thought I was about to beat this sucka up! If he takes too long, I will go in and get them myself. However, after a few minutes, the kids came out, looking tremendously nervous.

"Ok, here they go. When will they be back?" Reece's voice sounded a little shaky.

"We'll call you. Here's my card if you need to contact me." I responded.

The kids did not say a word in the car the entire ride to my office, even when I asked them if they were hungry. Reece must have scared them to make sure they would not talk. By the time we made it there, I already had some hot pizza delivered waiting just for them.

"It's all yours, kids. If you do not eat it, I'll just have to put it in the trash." I tried sounding as friendly as possible to show them they did not have to be afraid of me.

Sam looked at Samantha for confirmation before grabbing a slice. Once she gave him a head nod, that large pizza was almost gone within minutes.

"Oh, I almost forgot about your drinks. Do y'all want some juice?" I asked.

"Mmm-hmm!" they answered in unison, their mouths full of pizza.

As I gathered their drinks, I noticed Sam squirming in his seat. He wanted to say something. "What is your name again?" He asked.

Samantha nudged Sam's arm for breaking the code of silence and whispered in his ear, "Remember, don't talk!"

Even though she whispered, I read her lips. I knew if I wanted to get any information from them, I needed to separate the two, but with Samantha being the overprotective big sister, I knew that would be hard to do.

"It's okay, Sam. Call me Ms. Anders. Do you guys know why I brought you here?"

"Yeah, is it because you want us to tell you our secret?"

"That is right, Sam, you can tell me anything. I will keep you safe—"

"We are not talking!" Samantha shouted.

"Why not, Samantha? You don't think I'll keep you safe?"

"It's just that… if we talk, Uncle Reece will be really angry at us and he's going to do bad things," Samantha said as she was tearing up.

Sam started crying softly, and Samantha put her arm around him like a protective big sister.

I looked both in the eyes. "Samantha—"

She interrupted me. "Can you call me Sammy? That's what Dad used to call me before he left."

She was opening a little, but she still had her guard up. "Ok, Sammy. Remember, I can protect you. If you tell me what's going on…."

As Sammy took a deep breath and opened her mouth to talk, I heard a knock on the door. "Um, hold on, guys. I'll be right back."

It was James, my boss. He had a disappointed look on his face. I am usually excited to see him since he's sweet in my eyes, but I know at this moment it wasn't good.

I stepped out into the hallway to receive the bad news.

"Oh no, what's wrong?" I folded my arms, knowing I would not like what he was going to say.

"Their mother is here with a lawyer. They're demanding to see the kids and take them home."

"Wait! Samantha was just about to tell me everything!" I knew James saw the anger on my face.

"I know, it's bullshit, Journey, but we still have to let them sit in with the children during questioning."

I instantly dropped my head. "I see. Ok, James."

When I went back to the room and told the kids their mother was there, they did not seem too excited. I moved them to the conference room and let them have a moment to speak with their mother and lawyer. By the time I came in to gather a statement from them, they said they had made everything up. They stated that they only said those things because their uncle punished them for not doing their chores and had taken away their video games.

"I'm sorry for wasting your time, Ms. Anders. I will deal with my children once we get home, but I assure you that my brother did not do any of those God-forsaken things that they said." She spoke.

I could not believe what I was hearing. Their mother's mannerisms were completely off, as if she were trying to sound believable. I could tell she was lying. She even declined to let the children get examined to check for any sexual abuse. I wanted to cry right then because I just knew Reece was sexually abusing the kids, but without the children's confession, I had no proof.

After ignoring their mother, I looked the kids right in the eyes before I spoke. "Are you sure nothing happened? Nobody will be mad; just tell the truth, and I will protect you. Did your uncle hurt you?"

"Ms. Anders, I am their lawyer, and these children have given their statement already. Let us not badger them with these questions again. Mr. Whitman is innocent. He did nothing to them. If there is nothing else, you have no legal obligation to keep them here. They are free to go."

I wondered how much this lawyer was being paid and even if he had a soul. As they were leaving, Sammy looked back at me when nobody was looking and nodded her head and motioned her mouth, 'yes'. I knew she wouldn't admit it to the lawyer or the mother. The mother may have already known. I had to do something; I would not let this case end up like Cindy's case, but what could I do? On one hand, I had to follow protocol, and on the other, I could not let these children get hurt anymore. While at home, I put on my black hoodie and my grappling gloves. I could feel it in my gut. Reece was going to hurt them tonight. I drove over to their house, parked across the street, and waited. It was after eleven o'clock. Not sure of what I was waiting for, I just sat there.

After ten minutes of waiting, I was about to start up my car and leave when a bedroom light came on. The driveway was empty, so that only meant their mother was not home. I stepped out of my car and ran to the window. There was a spot in between the blinds where I could look in. I saw Reece in boxers with no shirt on, arguing with Sammy. Sam was in the corner, trembling in fear, crying. Suddenly, Reece put Sammy in a chokehold, started kissing her and threw her on the bed. I completely lost it, broke the bedroom window, and crawled in. Between the kids screaming and crying, I did not care if anyone heard me come in, but I tried to be as discreet as possible.

When I came in, Reece was completely naked, standing over Sammy, trying to take her clothes off. All I saw was red. I rushed over behind Reece and punched him several times in the back of his head. He slumped over in pain. Sammy got up and ran to her brother. While Reece was still bent over in agony, trying to figure out what was happening to him, I jumped in the air, spinning my body around, landing several kicks to his face. At that moment, he collapsed to the ground. I quickly leapt on his back, put my arm around his throat, and then squeezed as tight as I could. Reece started banging his hands on the ground as if we were in a wrestling competition, so I squeezed harder.

His hands started moving more slowly with the last brief life he had left. I glanced up and saw the look of horror on the kids' faces. So, I released my arms and got off him. He started gasping for air and pleaded for mercy. I regained my composure, bent down, and whispered in Reece's ear with a tight grip around his throat.

"Tell the cops everything you did to these kids. If you don't, I will find out and come back for you."

I made sure I did not let go until I knew he understood everything I said. After I knew we had a good understanding, I grabbed some extension cords that were lying nearby on the floor and tied him up. I then walked over to Sammy and Sam. At first, they seemed a little frightened. They were not sure if I was coming to hurt them next.

"Call the police, Samantha. Tell them everything. You are safe now." I tried to disguise my voice so they would not recognize me. Admittedly, I know I sounded crazy, but I could not risk getting exposed.

"Ok, who are you and how did you know my name?" Sammy started walking towards me.

"A superhero!" Sam screamed excitedly.

I rushed over to the window before she got closer to me. Sammy then grabbed the phone and called 911. After she made the call, I jumped out the window. I waited until the cops arrived before I drove away. The smile on my face could not get any bigger. I just could not believe I did that! I saved them—not Ms. Anders, but the superhero!

The next morning, it was all over the news. **HOODED HERO SAVES KIDS** was the headlines. I just could not believe it! Did they recognize me? What if they found out it was me? Will I get into trouble? So many thoughts raced through my head, and I did not know what to think or do. Then the phone rang...

"Hello?" I sounded so scared, not knowing who was on the phone.

"Hey, Journey, are you coming to work today? This is James. You were supposed to be here thirty minutes ago," he asked with a concerned tone.

"Oh, I'm sorry, James, and yes, I'm coming in today. I'm getting dressed right now. Sorry, I overslept!" I explained.

There was a slight silence before he asked the big question.

"Ok, well... I suppose you haven't seen the news yet?"

Nervously, I said, "News? No, why?"

"It's about Sam and Samantha..." He answered.

My heart skipped a beat. I must be careful with everything that I say next.

"What about them, James? Are they okay?" I asked.

"Well, their uncle confessed to everything. He has been hurting them for five years now and has given incredibly detailed information on everything he's done to them. Somebody caught him in the act and beat him up badly. They must have put a scare on him. Police bust through the doors and saw that somebody had tied him up, naked." He answered intensively.

"James, I do not feel bad about him being hurt, but his admission is a great thing for Sam and Samantha. Now we can move in the right direction to get them removed from their uncle and begin the healing process." I replied.

I really could not believe he did everything I told him to do.

"I know, I know… well, hurry and come in so I can give you all the details." He said.

"Thanks, James. On my way!"

When I arrived at work, the 'hooded hero' seemed to be the discussion that everyone was having. I cannot blame them, though; I beat him up badly. When I made it to my office, I was very relaxed with my feet kicked up on my desk, and my arms were gently across my head when someone opened my office door, interrupting my relaxation.

It was James.

"You're late and you're not working? What's gotten into you lately?" he asked angrily.

Quickly moving my feet and sitting up; "I'm so sorry again, James, I'm just super happy for Sam and Samantha!"

"I know we all are, but we still have work to do. We must find them a home."

"A home? What's wrong with their mother?" I asked.

James dropped his head down, then sighed. "She knew about it all along. She said what her brother did was not that bad because her father did the same thing to her when she was younger, so it wasn't a big deal."

"What a sick, twisted family!" I uttered.

"Right. Police are looking to charge her also, and after looking over this police report, the hooded hero should've killed him and their mother. It's extremely bad."

Do not tell me that, James, because I will go back and finish the job!

"James, any word on this hero?"

"No. Nobody came forward yet, police are just thinking somebody who knew Kung Fu was walking by and heard the children screaming, then jumped in and saved them."

I started looking at James strangely as he motioned his hands, doing karate chops.

"Anyhow, I have everything ready for you in their files, including the police report. The children are at the hospital now. Two relatives are saying they want them, so start looking into it."

"I'm on it, James!"

After what took almost an entire week, I finally found a suitable home for Sam and Samantha with a relative. The home that I thought would be great for them was in Galveston, Texas, with their aunt. Her kids were off to college and had empty rooms for them.

When I saw the kids, they were excited after I told them the news. They could not wait to be near the beach. After a few hours, the aunt finally arrived and embraced them with so much love. I know this was the right person for them. The kids told me bye, and Samantha looked back at me and said, "Thank you."

The next day, I stopped by Mom's house when I arrived. Thu was there as always.

"Hey Thu, sorry about missing training the other day." I wanted to say it first because I knew it was coming.

"Over ten years of training, you only missed a day if you were sick, or you were studying for school. You like some boy now?" He angrily asked.

I started laughing. "Thu, there's no boy, I don't have time for that right now in my life, and my schedule is crazy! I just got caught up with work. Sorry for not calling you."

"Hm. You hear about this hooded hero yet?" He sat down and picked up the newspaper. "All over the news."

"Yes, the kids involved were my clients. I thought the case was going to go sour, but whoever this hooded hero is, really saved them!" I tried sounding believable.

As I poured a cup of coffee and took a sip, I saw Thu giving me a stern look.

"Hey, baby! I didn't hear you come in!" My mom was happy and glowing like I had never seen before.

"Hey, Mom, just thought I'd stop by and see what you are up to."

"Oh, nothing, just doing laundry as always on Saturdays!" she said cheerfully.

Mom walked towards the laundry room to put another load in.

## *Whack!*

Thu hit me hard across the head with the newspaper he was reading.

"Heyyy!! Thu, what was that for?" I yelled while rubbing my head.

"I know it was you!" The look he had on his face was serious, and he meant business.

"What do you mean?" I asked.

"Hooded hero! Don't play dumb with me girl… this was you!"

"Shhh!! Ok, Ok! Be quiet, I don't want Mom to know!" I knew there was no point in lying.

"You still have learning to do. We will train tonight! Six o'clock, don't be late!" Thu said furiously.

From the look he had on his face, I knew he was not playing, but how did he even know?

Mom walked back into the room,

"You two training again? I thought you would get tired of it by now, but I'm so glad you can use karate to get your mind off everything. Oh, and did you know a hero is floating around us? Saved two babies the other day. Seen it on the news! I immediately thought of you… if only we had somebody like that, you know- a superhero or vigilante years ago, then maybe…"

Interrupting, I pleaded, "It is ok, Mom. Everything happens for a reason. I'm about to go home, quick, freshen up and change." While walking out the door, I looked back and said,

"Thu, I will meet you at the spot at six sharp!"

When I arrived, it was completely dark inside the building. It looked as though nobody was there.

"Thuuu I'm here. Where are you?" I yelled. I was not like him to not show up.

I instantly started hearing what sounded like two knives rubbing together…

"Thu is that you??"

I did not feel right, so I got into position, prepared to fight, just in case something was about to go down. Then I heard that sound again. After that, a flow of wind like someone just jumped over my head. They cut the straps of my backpack off, and it fell to the ground, but no one was in sight! I started kicking and throwing punches, but I touched nothing, and no one was around me. For the first time in a long time, I was frightened.

While laughing low and creepy, "I told you, you still have so much to learn!"

It was Thu! He slowly started walking towards me with a sword in each hand and had on this dark outfit that completely covered his entire body and mouth. All I saw were his eyes.

"Thu?! How did you, where did you...what???" I said, puzzled and intrigued at the same time.

"Lóng Quán is what they called me many years ago. It means Dragon Fist. I saved many people and stopped many crimes. No one knew of my identity—until now." He stated as he walked towards me.

So much ran through my mind, so many questions, but when I opened my mouth, nothing came out.

"Journey, I knew when I first started training you that -you were going to become something incredibly special. I am not The Almighty, but I believe this is your fate. This is your fire—your mission. This is what you've been training for!"

When he said that, a chill went through my body. I felt his words and knew he meant everything he was saying. This is something that I want and something that needs to be done; this day will never be forgotten because today is the day that I realized my purpose.

# Chapter Three

Create in me a pure heart, O God, and renew a right spirit within me. Psalms 51:10

*White:* *wholeness, purity, & radiance*

So much has happened since the day I found out who Thu *really* was. I want to find out more about Thu's past, but he does not want me to know more about him. So, I will give him his space for now and just focus on training. Thu strongly suggests that we train before and after work every day for two months. Each time I got tired when we trained, I thought about how I wanted to improve my skills. I wanted to help as many people as possible. I want to be every victim's voice, strength, and weapon. Still, I must stay in the shadows; because of what I do during the day, I can't let anyone find out who I am. Thu has been teaching me many new techniques and I feel like an entirely different person. My favorite thing out of all the fighting techniques that he taught me is called the kuzushi waza, or backwards trip. It's MMA fighting and karate together; a mixture of punching and tripping my opponents. This is one of the reasons why I love Thu so much; he has several fighting moves up his sleeve, but I can also tell his age is catching up to him. To add, we collaborated on a new idea together that I'm proud of. I have an outfit now! I wear it only during battle- no more hoodies for me. This African, cat woman, ninja-looking suit is more my vibe and more memorable.

I went back to work after taking three days off following Sam and Samantha's case. They thought I went on a quick vacation, but the training and pain I endured with Thu was no vacation!

"Journey! Nice to have you back with us. How was your vacation?"

James seemed kind of excited to see me.

While smiling, I said, "Hi James, it was nice, kind of wish it was longer."

James walked over to me and started hugging me.

"Aww, don't be like that. I know you are happy to be back saving these kids."

"Yes, that's the part I enjoy!" I said while looking into his eyes.

"Now we are talking! I have a file ready for you to look at on your desk. It's a new case that needs immediate attention. Let me know if you need any help."

The way he handed me the files was a little different. I don't know, maybe I was reading things wrong, but he was looking at me differently with his contagious smile. I was stuck there, smiling at him. James is 6'7, has smooth chocolate skin, is well educated, and is very muscular. He's also very single. I can only imagine the things he can do to me, at night, in my bed, under my covers, putting his fingers in my…

"Um. Journey, are you still there? Where did you go? I was talking to you, and you just drifted off. Still thinking about that vacation you were on?"

Blushing, I said, "Oh my gosh, I'm so sorry, James, thank you. I will look at these files right now!"

As he walked out of my office, James said, "Oh, okay, um, let me know if you need me."

"Ok, James, I will!" I replied blissfully.

I was so embarrassed before he even left the room, I covered my face with the files. Why was I acting like a little shy high schooler and not the Black queen I am? Maybe because he has all the characteristics that I like in a man, and even has a great sense of humor.

As I read the files with a smile on my face, it instantly disappeared the deeper I read. I started tapping my fingers on my desk and then felt my blood pressure rising. I was angry beyond belief. My education and work experience have taught me not to take anything personally and not to take my work home with me, but sometimes I can't help it. I cannot stand child abusers, and I demand justice!

## *[Knock-knock]*

"Hey James, sorry to disturb you, but I am a little confused. As I read the file, it states that Brian Matthews, nine years old, went to school with obvious signs of abuse; he is with a relative right now while we investigate his mother. But then it says that he has a twelve-year-old brother named Kevin whom nobody has seen for more than a year?! Why haven't the whereabouts of Kevin been investigated?

"I pondered that myself. It was one of those situations where Mom told the school that Kevin was now living with his biological dad. Brian has a different father from Kevin. When you were out, I tried to locate his father many times, but I am still unsuccessful. The mother is now saying that the father recently moved, and she does not have their current address. Brian has old and new bruises all over his body. I need you to talk to the mother." James looked genuinely concerned.

"Not feeling good about this one, James. According to the medical report, Brian's condition was severe. How do we know she did nothing to Kevin? Did Brian say what happened to him?" I asked.

Shaking his head, "He is not talking. He has not said one word to anybody since they took him out of the home."

"Poor baby is so scared that he won't talk," I said with a sigh of irritation. "Ok, I'll try to speak to Brian first, and then I'll talk to the mother."

With a controlled smile, James said, "Determination. Glad to see you back in action, I love it! Let me know if you need me."

I walked out... love seeing James so excited. It puts a smile on my face.

As I was on my way to check up on Brian, I just could not stop thinking about his brother, Kevin. 'I prayed this kid is okay. Hopefully, Brian can tell me his whereabouts.' As I approached the house, his aunt greeted me as if we were family.

"Hi, is Brian Matthew's home? I am his new social worker, Journey Anders."

"Oh, ok, yes. Hello, Journey. I am his aunt Brenda; I was told you were on your way over here. Come on in, you want some coffee?" She said cheerfully.

"No, thank you, I'm trying to cut that habit."

"Oh, I know what you mean. Maybe I should stop too… might even drop a couple of pounds! Well, Brian is in his room. Let me walk you back there."

"Thank you so much." Brenda reminds me so much of my family, so polite.

"Now, do not expect too much out of him, Ms. Journey. He's been silent since he got here. I don't know what happened at my Half-sister's house. She has been battling with life and has been taking her issues out on those babies! I am babbling. I'm so sorry. Follow me. I'll take you to Brian."

"No worries, I understand."

I feel her anger, and I can see that she cares about these boys. As I approached Brian in his room, he seemed extremely nervous and scared.

"Hi Brian, I have heard so much about you. I am here because I want to help you in any way that I can. My name is Journey Anders. You can call me Journey."

Brian took one look at me, then started back reading his book, *Call of the Wild*.

"Wow! Brian, this is an excellent book that you are reading. No matter how tough things have gotten, he pushed through and fought for survival. No matter how hard things got, he gave his all. *'With the last remnant of his strength'*…"

"Hey, that is in the story!" Brian stated.

"Yes, it is. I used to read it when I was a kid. Whenever I would feel down about a situation I was going through, I always read this book to help me overcome it."

"Well, did you get over it?" Brian seemed intrigued by what I said.

"I will never forget what happened to me, Brian, but I pushed past it. I survived."

Brian looked up at me. I do not even think he realized he was talking. His deep brown eyes watered, and his lips started shivering.

"I'M SCARED!" he shouted and suddenly burst into tears, then laid his head on my chest.

"I know this situation scares you, Brian. But I promise you are safe now. Can you tell me what happened to you and Kevin?"

"K-K-Kevinnnn!!!!!! He's gone!"

Just as Brian was about to pour out his guts and tell me everything, Brenda walked into the room. I knew I would not get much out of him now.

43

"He's talking! You got him to talk?!" I smiled at her and then returned to speaking to Brian.

"Hey, Brian, I will come back in a couple of days so we can finish our conversation. I want you to sit down and think about everything that has happened. I want you to tell me everything, ok?"

In a soft voice, he said, "Ok."

As tears rolled down his face, I handed him my card.

"If you want to talk sooner, you can call me anytime. You two have a great weekend."

I rushed to Brian's mother's house, even though he did not say it. I knew she hurt Brian and Kevin. I thought that somehow, I would get her to admit that she did something to them.

When I arrived, she was outside smoking on her porch, and her house looked like something you had seen in a horror movie. After I parked my car and walked closer, I instantly had an eerie feeling about her. I can admit, I understood why her sister said she looks like she's been battling with life. Just from the look of her face, her smell, dirty fingernails, unmatched clothing, and the torn-up shoes she was wearing. If I saw her on the street, I would assume she was homeless.

"Hello, Teresa Matthews?"

"Yes, I'm Teresa. Who are you?" She sounded like she wasn't interested in talking to me, but I tried sounding as caring as possible.

"Hi, I'm Journey Anders. I'm with Child Protective Services. I have your son, Brian, as my client."

As I tried to shake her hand, she just looked at it and then rolled her eyes as she took another puff of what smelled like marijuana.

"No worries, Ms. Matthews, I'm no cop. I…"

"I know you're not a damn cop, so what the fuck do you want? With yo corny ass!"

Trying to remain professional, I ignored the fact that she cut me off and continued talking.

"Ms. Matthews…"

She stopped me by blowing smoke in my face and then shouted, "It's Teresa, BITCH!"

Stay calm, Journey.

"Listen, Teresa. I am trying to speak to you about Brian, but you are being difficult. So, I am just going to get right to it. Why did you beat him?"

While laughing, Teresa said, "I am so sorry to inform you, but Brian has always been weak. The poor boy is extremely clumsy as well. Just like I told the police, he fell. He fell down the stairs and went to school crying and whining… making everybody feel sorry for him. Anything else, Ms. Anderson?"

She did not have a care in the world and was taking everything like it was a joke. I felt sorry for her boys because they had to live with her.

"Yes, there is one more thing. Where's Kevin?" I looked her directly in her eyes. She seemed a little surprised and began smoking again.

"He is with his daddy, and before you ask, I don't know their new address. Now step off my property. I have some packing to do." She barked.

With a confused look, I asked, "Oh, you're moving?"

"Look. Yes! I am moving, and yes, I gave the new address to the detectives. I got evicted, so unless you want to help me move, then leave my property before I make you leave!"

Teresa stood up and got in my face. I looked up at her with a stare that instantly let her opposing frame know I was not afraid of her. Once I knew she understood that, I walked to my car.

"I'll keep in touch, Ms. Matthews. Oh, and it's Anders, not Anderson." I smiled at her, then got in my car.

She flicked her smoke on the porch, gave me the finger, and shouted, "WHATEVER SKANK!" as I drove off.

Later that night, my phone rang at three o'clock in the morning. After ignoring it the first time, it started ringing again.

Angrily, I answered the call from this unknown number.

"Hello!?"

"Um… miss-miss. Journey?" He said in a scared tone.

I could tell it was a kid talking.

"Yes? This is she? Who's this?" I replied.

"Um… this is Brian." He answered. "Do you want me to call you tomorrow? I'm ready now."

"No, Brian, you can talk to me right now. It's okay. You want to tell me what happened to you?" I was extremely eager, but I did not want to seem pushy.

"Yes, but I'm scared that if I tell you, she will hurt me and you."

Clearing my throat, "Brian, you are safe. I will let nothing happen to you- or me. I will protect you!"

He exclaimed, "My mom is not a nice person. My mom hits me all the time. She says I am a demon… that is why she pushed me down the stairs. She was trying to kill me because she said the demon that was in Kevin's body was now in my body, so she needed to kill me. I am so scared!!!" Brian cried.

"Brian, Brian, it's ok… I will make sure she will never touch you again! Where is Kevin?" I questioned.

He mumbled, "At her house…"

"No, Brian, he's not there. I went to your mom's house yesterday." I explained.

"He's in the house. He has always been in the house. Mom made sure she kept a close eye on him," he whispered.

"Brian..." Before I could finish my sentence, Brian interrupted.

"Check the freezer," he mumbled.

A long chill ran through my body as I listened to the dial tone. Check the freezer? Is he saying what I think he's saying? Should I involve the police? That is what I'm supposed to do, but I do not want to call the cops. I just want to go over there myself to make sure it's handled correctly. I can't have another case like Cindy Adams. Justice needs to be served for Brian and Kevin, so I will make sure it happens!

It took me 20 minutes to gear up and make it to Teresa's house. All the lights were off, and they parked a moving truck outside the house, which only meant that she was inside. As I checked all the doors and windows, I finally snuck in from the back window that was left unlocked. I quietly tiptoed throughout the house, assuming she was in the bedroom, asleep. I made my way into the kitchen, opened the freezer, and nothing was there other than ice cream and dead roaches. Confused, I wandered around a little more just to see if I could find anything.

The house smelled terrible, and it was a complete mess. She was a hoarder. There were piles of garbage in the house that seemed like they had been there for years.

I could not believe the children were living under these conditions, and to be abused on top of it all was heartbreaking just to think about. As I walked around more, I entered the living room and stepped on something by the couch. I thought it was trash, but when I turned around, I saw eyes beaming up at me. It was Teresa; she was lying on top of trash on the couch, and I accidentally stepped on her foot.

"WHO THE FUCK ARE YOU??" she yelled furiously.

I must admit, it threw me off a little, but I was ready for anything that would happen next. As she tried standing up, I spotted a deep freezer behind the couch. I grabbed the back of her head and kneed her face; she collapsed on the floor. I made my way to the freezer and opened it; there he was, wrapped in plastic, stuffed in the freezer.

She murdered her son!

By that time, Teresa was back standing up and somehow had a crowbar in her hand. She took a swing at me. I shielded myself with my forearms. I used that moment to lunge towards her, wrestling the crowbar from her grasp. While straddling her, I started strangling her with the visual of Kevin's body on my mind. While gasping for air, Teresa was frantically kicking and moving her arms up and down, searching for an object to hit me with. I am not a killer, so I eased off her. She started breathing heavily and put her hand gently around her throat while trying to regain composure.

"Why? Who are you?" Teresa asked while struggling to speak.

As I looked at the freezer, then glanced back at her, I instantly became furious all over again. I grabbed the front of Teresa's shirt, then brought her face closer to mine and shouted, "This is for Kevin and Brian!"

With a balled fist, I struck her in the face, knocking her out. I called the police after tying her up and giving them enough details of the crimes that this monster committed, and leaving trails of the evidence needed. I left the house the same way I came in and did not leave until the cops arrived.

## The next day...

As I was walking into James' office, he was hanging up the phone.

"Hello, James, sorry to be busting through your office like this so early in the morning, but I have something extremely important to tell you!" gushed my sing-songy voice.

"Really? Because I have some news for you as well, but let me hear what you have to say first." James seemed eager to talk, so I am guessing the news is already out about Teresa.

"Ok, well, it's about Brian. He called and told me everything. According to him...there is a body, James." I tried to sound as convincing as possible.

"Sadly, there *is* a body." He said with sadness. "However, Teresa is in custody as we speak!" He was so excited that he started shaking my shoulders.

Okay, James, keep shaking me like that, and I might accidentally let a boob pop out.

'I am so glad you cannot hear my thoughts.'

"Oh, wow! That is great James. I did not know! Her kids will get the justice they deserve." I tried sounding like I was shocked as much as possible.

"Journey, this lady is very twisted. She confessed to everything but then said she had to do it, she had to kill them because they were being possessed by demons. She was more concerned about some woman breaking into her house, beating her up."

"Hmm… I'm no psychologist, but maybe she's suffering from some type of mental illness. It's a shame nobody noticed her actions towards them or even noticed Kevin missing. Now Brian has to grow up without his brother." I added.

James started pacing back and forth with his hands on top of his head, as if he was stressed.

"I'm not so sure that she was completely nuts when she said some woman beat her up. I mean, the police said somebody knocked her out. When she opened her eyes, the cops were already there. This is the same scenario with Sam and Samantha with the hooded hero.

We may have a vigilante on our hands! How else would you explain Teresa being tied up and beaten?"

It thrilled James at the thought of having a vigilante and finally having some help with getting these cases solved.

"Wait, I don't know James. I'm sure the police would have mentioned this if that were the case. I mean, Dallas having a real vigilante, or some type of superhero, sounds too good to be true." I tried not to sound too sarcastic.

"From the looks of the people she put her hands on... I'm thinking she's very well trained." James responded.

After the conversation with James, I left to check up on Brian. He was relieved that everyone knew about what happened to Kevin and was happy his mom was in jail. This case made me feel like I could do anything, and no one would ever find out I was the one behind the mask. I was invisible. Brian was safe with his aunt and the image of Kevin's body well... his bones will never leave my mind; I could not protect him, but at least Brian was somewhere safe. A couple of months passed, my secret identity had solved several cases, and every time I would draw an ankh somewhere to let everyone know it was me. That symbol showed my lifelong commitment to protecting children from predators. With each case, I got stronger and stronger and saved many lives; I helped Anthony Young get a permanent home away from his abusive and alcoholic father. Thirteen-year-old Dennis Hollow couldn't stop crying after I pulled him out of a locked closet where he had been contained for two years by his stepmother and biological father. He weighed only eighty pounds and had obvious signs of physical abuse. Amber Johnson didn't even look back, as I nearly killed the man who held her captive as a sex slave for several years. Her case brought me to tears because they had had her since she was a toddler. Now she's a teenager. All she knows is that traumatic life experience. Many other cases that were solved by the person they call, Bast.

# Chapter Four

So do not fear, for I am with you; do not be dismayed, for I am your God. I will strengthen you and help you; I will uphold you with my righteous right hand. Isaiah 41:10

*Blue:* *represents freedom, inspiration, confidence, & faith*

That day, after Thu revealed his secret identity to me, or who he used to be, a lot changed. He gave me a name and purpose; I cannot stop what I started, and I cannot leave any boy or girl with people who are hurting them. Every battle that I fight makes a difference to the case I am solving and to other kids who are in similar situations. I want my name to give every child hope who is going through tough situations, and I want my name to be known to pedophiles. My goal is to make my name stop them from attempting to cause harm to children. If that doesn't work, they won't have a fighting chance of escaping from me once I capture them.

The conversation I had with Thu the night he revealed his secret will never leave me.

"Journey, you are a fierce warrior who moves swiftly without making a sound. Bast was a protective goddess, just like you; you can't sit still knowing that a child is being harmed. You try your best to protect them, even if that means putting your own life in jeopardy and risking everything! Therefore, your name should be Bast; in ancient Egyptian history, people worshipped Bast, and she was well-loved. She was the goddess of the sun, who later changed into the cat goddess. You are a docile student. That makes you extremely powerful! You're always willing to learn more and master whatever is brought to you!" Explained Thu.

"Badass Bastet! Kickin' butt and movin' just like a cat, but don't be mistaken cus she ain't no pet!" I rapped. "Ok, I like that name, Thu!" I had to jump in and interject what I thought would be a great theme song or rap for my commercial.

The look on Thus' face was showing me he was not in a laughing mood. He looked angry.

"Forgive me, I'm very sorry, Thu! I was kidding. I seriously love the name and feel honored to be named after a goddess!"

Angrily, Thu spoke, "For many people, she was so much more than a goddess. This is a name that deserves much respect. She is a protector! Study lions and learn how to mimic their behavior! Now!"

Thu never got that serious with me before. I didn't want to disappoint him. This must have meant a lot to him.

For the next several months, all I did was study Bastet and lionesses as much as I ate and slept. Just thinking about it gave me chills! I am shocked that Thu did not want my name to be some ancient Chinese warrior. I guess Thu understands me better than I know myself. He knows what I would like. When I trained, Thu would always shout: "Hunt, protect, nurture!" From now on, that motto will be in my head with every case that I close. When I get a case, I will hunt or search determinedly and pursue the predator. I will keep everyone that I am protecting safe from injury and harm. I will also forever stay connected with every person whom I save and try to encourage, as well as mentor them. My goal is to have each kid grow up and be successful, and not to allow their past to affect their future.

For a while, everything seemed to have been working out perfectly, but nothing truly prepared me for my next case. I was finally at a point in my life where I felt untouchable. I was solving cases like clockwork and felt like no one could stop me from getting rid of some of the scum that is floating around Dallas, Texas. It still feels weird that I am keeping the one thing that is bringing me so much joy away from my mother. We have a close relationship, but I cannot let her know about Bast; she would not understand. When I call my mom to talk about any situation that I am in, she always finds a way to involve God. Not saying that's a bad thing, but sometimes she can go a bit overboard. I don't care if I am talking to her about needing advice for medical, love, depression, money, or even sex. She will have bible verses prepared and ready for me, then will expect me to read them to her regardless of the time or the day. That's my mother, and I love her deeply. It was these types of conversations that will stick with me and will be useful with the next challenges that will approach me.

Back at work, I was in my office when James came rushing in. His eyes were wide as if someone had spooked him.

"What's wrong, James?" I asked.

"Do you remember a case you had sometime last year with a girl named Ebony Thomas, 12 years old, raped repeatedly by mom's boyfriend, Tom Adams?" James' voice was very shaky. I had never seen him act like this before.

"Yeah, yeah, I think so… the girl that had to be put in protective custody, right?"

I knew exactly who he was talking about because I nearly killed the man who was raping her. Ebony's story reminded me too much of my story when I was a kid.

"Yes! Well…" James grabbed my hands and then continued, "They found her dead!"

I immediately broke free from his hands. "WHAT! WHAT HAPPENED??" I asked.

James dropped his head and said, "Her body was naked and disemboweled in the middle of the street. Police said that she is the second kid they have found like that. They do not have enough evidence yet, but it is rumored that Ebony was murdered by a group called MCLA."

All I saw was red. I felt my blood pressure rising.

"MCLA? I am confused. What is that? Disemboweled?" I shouted.

"Man Child Love Association. A group of pedophiles started from another country. They are trying to have sex with kids legally. Police just found out about this and got a hit on one of their associates. They found out that the man who raped Ebony was a member. The police are saying MCLA found out where

Ebony was and did this to her, possibly because they were afraid she would name names."

"James, where is Tom now?"

James dropped his head again, "You didn't hear?? Tom escaped from prison three weeks ago, and police are searching for him now."

"Why wasn't I told about this? I could've protected her!" I cried.

James started walking towards me, trying to console me, but I turned around.

"Journey, there's a limit to our job. There's only so much we can do to save these kids. It is in the police's hands now. They were supposed to protect her, but they failed. To top it off, there's more..." James seemed a little unsure about continuing.

Turning around, "There's more, James?" I was uncertain if I could manage more bad news.

"Much more. On the side of Ebony's face, they drew the Ankh symbol on her cheek with a black marker, then a huge X was over it, made with her blood. Police are saying this was a killing intended to catch Bast's attention. Maybe it's a warning for her to stay away," explained James.

Speechless, confused, and hurt, James allowed me to take the rest of the day off to let everything register for what happened to Ebony. He knew I had gotten close to her; I had never broken down with any case before, but this case has me torn. Ebony was so sweet and innocent; she only told her mom that Tom was raping her because her mom asked her if something was going on after sensing strange behavior from her. She didn't want to lie to her mother. Ebony was in protective custody because Tom's friends kept threatening Ebony and her mother after they sentenced Tom. Ebony was in a safe and secluded area. There's no way they could have found out where she was, which makes me believe MCLA is bigger than they think.

For the next several weeks, I did research on MCLA, and I found out that it originated in China. This organization was trying hard to make it legal to have sex with children. They were protesting and talking to big names to make this law pass; they said that we need this law to pass so parents can stop hurting children when they find out they have an inappropriate relationship with an adult. This organization's argument was that if the law can make same-sex relationships legal, then what is the difference between having a relationship with a minor or an animal? This argument is laughable, but there were more people in favor of this law than I realized. I made sure Bast laid low for now. I had to make smart moves because I couldn't have anyone else hurt.

My days were quiet at work, and I had not been checking up on Mom like I usually do. I had even been ignoring Thu's phone calls. I was depressed and just wanted to be left alone. This was not my usual character,

Journey and Bast were both being attacked at the same time, and I didn't know how to handle it. I knew I needed to hurry up and figure out something soon before someone else could get hurt.

The following Friday, I had a knock on my door after I came home from work. When I opened it, I was so surprised that I did not speak.

"What's happenin' Kinfolk?!" he yelled energetically.

It was my cousin, Greg. He was my cousin on my father's side and had been in prison for a few years. I was told that he shot a man in self-defense, but because he had a record already and had a gun that was not registered, he had to serve time. I am not even sure if the man died, but when I found out he was in prison, I started writing to him a lot, and I'm pretty sure that's how he got my address. Greg was thirty-seven and very smart. His skills were with computers; he could do anything with technology. I never understood why he never used his talents to do something more productive instead of using them on the streets.

"Greg! When did you get out?" I asked while hugging him.

"Jay, they just let me out. Sorry to invade your space, but I had nowhere else to go. Can I stay here a while until I get on my feet?" He asked.

I let Greg in and allowed him to stay with me. I did not mind because he's great company to have around, and Greg is a protector. When he first found out what happened to me when I was younger, his exact words were, *'I am glad those motherfuckers are dead. If I had known, I would've killed them myself!'* Greg was extremely strong but thin. He's maybe 5'9 and wore a patch over his right eye. While he stayed with me, he told me his side of the story.

Greg was talking to a girl whom he met on a dating app. This girl was newly divorced from her abusive husband and had two children who were still in elementary school. After dating for a couple of months, Greg went over to the girl's apartment to hang out with them, not knowing the ex-husband had been stalking them and had a restraining order placed on him. Before he knew it, the ex-husband broke into the apartment and placed a gun to Greg's head. All Greg remembers is hearing one gunshot and then waking up in a hospital two days later, getting news that the ex-husband shot him in the eye and doctors had to remove it. Hearing that he'd wear an eye patch for the rest of his life wasn't the most devastating news they told him. It was the fact that the ex-husband also killed his ex-wife and kids and then fled from the scene before the police arrived. Two years after the tragedy happened, the killer was never caught, but somehow found out that Greg was still alive after shooting him in the face and decided to return to town to finish the job. Greg was able to get him first as he tried to take him out. Greg felt bad that he had died. He began tearing up while telling me his story, but he did not have a choice. If Greg did not kill him, then he would be dead right now.

Greg has been staying with me for a couple of weeks now. I must admit that he was the distraction that I needed because I kept thinking about MCLA and Ebony, but mostly, Tom stayed on my mind. I still can't believe he killed Ebony and then got away with it. "Where is he?" I mumbled.

"Where is who?" Greg said, with a confused look on his face.

"Oh, nothing. I was just thinking aloud. Sorry, I am having no fun right now. I usually go to my mom's house over the weekend, but I don't feel like making that drive," I confessed.

I tried to push the conversation as far away from Tom as possible.

"Jay, she's only forty-five minutes away, with traffic! I will drive us. It has been years since I saw her, anyway. Where are your keys?" Greg held his hands out, motioning for my keys.

I knew I could not talk him out of it, so I gave him my keys and we left.

As soon as we got there, Mom hugged us both for what seemed like hours. I did not see Thu. This shocked me.

"Mom, where's Thu?" I asked.

She dropped her head like she was about to give me terrible news. "He left after I told him you and Greg were coming over. He is just upset that he has not heard from you, and I don't blame him!" She snapped as she held her spatula.

"Mom…" I sat down and explained everything to her. I told her about Ebony, Tom, and MCLA. I told her how upset I was for not saving her, and I felt like this was all my fault.

"Jay, this is not your fault. You could not save her. You're only a social worker, not a superhero!" said Greg.

"I could have done more!" I cried.

Mom sat down next to me and grabbed my shoulders. "Baby, the world can be a cold and dark place. That is why we have people like you to be a light that guides us. A light that warms us. Everybody can't do what you do, and you do it very well. Just focus on doing what is right. God will handle the rest! I know the weight of these problems can be hard to bear, so find your peace, baby. Just know you will always have me and Thu on your side." She said while wiping my tears and hugging me.

I'm thankful for my mom's comfort. I need to get out there and do something about this.

I need to find Thu; I am ready to confront my problems instead of hiding from them, and I know exactly where Thu would be. The warehouse!

"Mom, Greg, I will be right back," I announced.

When I arrived, Thu was sitting down reading the newspaper and did not bother looking up when I said hello.

Apologetically, I said, "I am sorry for everything. I needed time to process the whole thing that had happened to me. One of my clients..."

"You are weak!" Thu said furiously after throwing his newspaper down and cutting me off. "You do not give up when things get hard! Your mother called and told me everything. This is the time to fight harder, not give up!"

"Thu, I've experienced nothing like this before. I haven't cried like this in a very long time... Ebony's head, Thu!" I said with tears rolling down my face. "What about you? How can you be hard on me right now? Have you ever been through something like this before?" I asked.

Thu got up and started pacing back and forth with his hands behind his back.

"Yes. I have, Journey." He whispered.

He told me to sit down and began telling me his story.

"When we first met, I told you I never experienced my mother's love as an adult because they took her from me when I was a kid. When I said 'they', I was talking about MCLA. They killed my mother and cut her head off." He explained.

I sat in shock as he continued his story; When he lived in China, he witnessed his mother's death at ten. One member of that group tried to take him, but his mother intervened. MCLA is trying to show the world that they are good people trying to make every relationship legal, but they are also kidnapping children, making them their sex slaves behind closed doors. When his mother stopped the kidnapping from happening, that is when they killed her. Thu ran away and never returned. After a while, a guy rescued him as soon as he saw him sleeping on the streets. He took him in as his own and trained him for years. That is how Lóng Quán was developed. He rescued people who needed help, and many of them were children who were victims of MCLA.

"Journey, when I first met and trained you, I said you were going to become something incredibly special. I am not the Almighty that we serve, but I feel like this is your destiny, your fire, and your mission in life; your past is your fire. It gave you a reason to fight and help others. This is what you have been training for! I did not know MCLA was going to enter your life. I thought I ended them in China, but I did not. They are growing because I failed." He lectured.

"I can't be weak anymore; I want to continue your legacy and bring MCLA down for good. I think I know where to start!" I said eagerly.

Thu's testimony was the motivation I needed to get back on track. We trained for the rest of the night. I can never give up so easily when things do not go as planned. Before I left, Thu handed me a dusty box.

"What is this?" I asked.

"Shoushan was my trainer who also grew to be a father to me. He raised me as his own child and taught me many lessons. Before he passed away from cancer, he gave this to me. Many generations have handed this box down, and now I am giving this to you!" Thu said with a gentle smile on his face.

I slowly opened the box and then gasped when I saw what someone had perfectly placed inside it.

"Qi Xing Long Yuan. It means the sword of integrity. This is ideal for you because of who you are and what you stand for. I want you to have it, put it up somewhere safe and cherish it." Declared, Thu.

As I stood there with tears in my eyes, admiring this beautiful sword, I softly placed it on the table next to me and hugged Thu. When I released him and looked up, I noticed his eyes were watering. I have never seen this side of him before. When Thu noticed me looking at him, he quickly wiped his tears away and took a step back.

Motioning his hands and clearing his throat, Thu said, "I have one more thing to give you. Please give me one more hour!"

"One more hour? Thu, it is already after midnight, and I know Mom is upset because she wanted me to look through the photo album with her again." While I was talking, Thu handed me two long wooden batons that were painted black.

"Why are you giving me batons?" I asked.

Smiling, he answered, "These are Escrima sticks used in the Filipino martial arts, used for fighting, comparable to sword fighting, but safer. I want you to use these each time you fight."

"So, let me get this straight. You gave me a sword, but you want me to use batons to beat people up? Seems odd to me." I said with a confused look on my face.

"Journey Anders, you funny girl, I do not want you to kill, although I want you to leave a mark on people that deserve it. Let me show you how dangerous these batons can be." He laughed.

Thu jumped up and started moving his hands fast while holding the batons. The different techniques he used were mind-blowing! He was tossing and chucking the batons with a powerful force. It only made me imagine somebody's face on the other side of the batons.

Thu explained to me that this technique is impacted by the length and weight of my baton and my ability from training to effectively strike with a baton. He instilled in me that personal power development is made up of my strength and my ability to manipulate the baton to deliver the most intense knockdown power. He kept repeating that power development begins with my strength. I know this only means that I can expect a lot more strength training tonight.

"Hunt, protect, nurture! Are you ready to train?" He shouted.

Smiling, I replied, "I am ready, Thu."

We trained, then we trained again.

He made sure I understood that I was training to injure, not kill. I can also use my baton for introducing pain to simply gain control. He said when using the baton to induce pain, aim for the meaty part of the body, the thighs, or arms. Make sure that I give hard, intense, full swings and swing all the way through, back and forth several times. He made sure that I understood that this was a less-than-lethal defensive technique, but to make sure it is not lethal, I had to make sure I never swung toward the face or head. He gave me a lot of techniques to use while fighting with batons. I think I will enjoy fighting with batons; it is an extra bang to go along with my punch.

# Chapter Five

There is a pathway that seems right to a man,
but in the end, it is a road to death.
Proverbs 14:1

**Brown:** *represents resilience, security, &
safety*

When I arrived back at Mom's house to pick Greg up the next morning, it was a little awkward since she was looking forward to me going over the photo album with her, but she understood. Greg just stared strangely at me the entire ride back to my place.

Furiously, I asked, "Greg! What is it? Why are you staring at me?"

"Are you and that old Chinese man bumpin' uglies?" he asked bluntly.

"Huh? What are you talking about? Speak English!" I yelled.

Laughing, he responded slowly like I was illiterate, "Are you and noodles in a relationship?"

I snapped, "Number one: you are racist. Number two: ew. Thu is like a father to me."

"Then why were you out all night with him?" He taunted. "It disappointed your mother."

"I know she wanted to spend some type of quality time with me, and I understand that, but I will do that at another time. There is something that I need to take care of right now." I stated.

"Are you in some type of trouble?" He asked.

"Maybe not." I grinned. "Before you went to prison, I remember you were really into computers. You used to do many things on your computer; you were very techy. Are you still like that?"

"Am I? If the cops were smart, I would have gone to prison for a lot more." He teased.

I took that as the opportunity to explain MCLA to him. I wanted him to look up a list of names that Thu gave me and find their whereabouts. Most of them should be old, living in China, or dead, but I hope we get lucky. Greg was more accepting than I thought. In fact, he was eager. He asked many questions and wanted to make sure I was safe and out of trouble. He knows how much Ebony meant to me.

Monday came, and I rushed to work trying to make it on time. I feel like I am getting nowhere with this case. When I arrived, a few of my co-workers were looking at me strangely. I thought it was odd, but I just ignored it and mumbled 'hi' under my breath, then went straight into my office. So much was on my mind. I could not sit down, so I paced back and forth. All I could think about was MCLA and destroying them.

"I'm going to destroy these bastards!" I yelled out loud.

## "Surprise!"

Amid me shouting and waving my fist in the air, positioned to fight. I turned around and saw James holding a birthday cake while my other co-workers held balloons. It was my birthday; I forgot all about it.

"Um. Ms. Anders, what are you doing?" James asked.

While embarrassed, I immediately started pulling down my shirt and regained my posture.

"Oh, I was playing a game on my phone, and I was celebrating my win!" I replied.

My office erupted in a roar of laughter, and then everyone took a slice of my cake after James said we could have a quick fifteen-minute break. I could not help gazing at James as he gulped down a slice of cake. The way he chewed was sexy, and I just realized he called me by my last name instead of Journey. I wonder why. As everyone started leaving my office, I walked over to James while he was cleaning his face with a paper towel.

"Cake for breakfast? You know it is only nine o'clock in the morning, right?" I said in a seducing way.

James chuckled and asked, "What is the difference between a cake and a doughnut?"

"Ha-ha, you are right, there's no difference." Clearing my throat, I walked over to him and asked, "By the way, why did you call me Ms. Anders a second ago? You usually say my first name."

"Oh, I did not know you didn't like me to be professional. Do you forgive me, Journey?" He grabbed my hands and placed them in the center of his chest while poking his bottom lip out. "Please forgive me, Journey." He pleaded.

A sudden rush of excitement rushed through my body as I felt his manly chest. James better stop tempting me. I am trying hard to remain professional.

"It is ok, really!" I giggled.

I slowly moved my hand down his chest, getting a quick feel of his masculinity. I stepped back a little and placed my hands down to my side. My body was getting a little too excited.

"Ok, I just want to make sure you are happy!" He said with a smile on his face. I think he knew I purposely got a quick feel of him, and he liked it.

"I am thrilled, Mr. Walker. Thank you for everything!" We both laughed.

"You got jokes. Ha-ha. Now, get back to work, and no more playing games on your phone!" He exclaimed as he left.

After James left, Mom popped into my mind. This was the reason she wanted me to go over the photo album with her. My birthday was coming up. This was a tradition of hers every year. Been so focused on everything else that has gone on in my life that I did not even realize my birthday was coming up. I am a terrible daughter; I need to call her. As I picked up my phone to call, it rang. It was Greg.

"Greg? You know I am at work."

"Jay! I found something!" Greg said with excitement.

"What? What did you find? Wait a minute, let us not talk about this over the phone. I will head home during my lunch break. Tell me everything you found!" I demanded.

"Ok, it's big, Jay." He paused. "Prepare yourself because this is sick! Very, very, sick!" He said in disgust.

"I will be home in two hours!" I shrieked.

Several minutes after hanging up, I kept watching the clock. It just seemed as if it was not moving fast enough! Fortunately, James had me doing paperwork for the moment, but I am extremely distracted. I need to see if he will let me off early.

Without hesitation, I ran straight to his office and opened the door.

"James, I apologize for busting into your office like this, but I need to ask you a favor!"

After straightening his tie in slow motion, he cleared his throat, then slowly licked his lips and said, "I am getting used to you bursting through my doors now…what is this favor? Could it be time off for your birthday?"

Trying to get back focused after my awkward hallucination, I replied, "My mom really wants to spend time with me since I ditched her this past weekend. I do not want to disappoint her again."

"Alright, alright, you can take the rest of the day off, but you must go with me to do a welfare check tomorrow morning. Deal?" He asked.

Is he blushing? He even stuttered a little bit; I think he may have a thing for me.

"Of course, it is a deal! I will see you first thing in the morning!" I shouted.

I anxiously ran to my car; I could not wait to see what Greg found for me. I made it home ticket-free. I was sure I was going to get pulled over with all the speeding I was doing. As I started jiggling with my keys on my door, trying to unlock them, I dropped the keys to the floor.

"Calm down, Journey!" I yelled. I gave it another try to open it. Why is it so dark?

"Greg?"

When I turned the light on, everybody jumped up from hiding.

## *"Surprise!"*

Not again. There were fifteen of my family members inside my apartment, and Greg was hiding in the corner with his hands over his face. Don't try to hide, I will deal with you later!

"Mom! Did you set all of this up?"

"Sure did, baby; I woke up this morning with you on my mind. I knew you were too busy with work stuff, so I called everyone to come right over! Good thing Greg is here. I don't know how I would have done this without him!" Mom said as she hugged me.

I glared over at Greg.

"I was not expecting you until later. You took off early?" Mom asked.

"Yes, my boss let me take the rest of the day off, but enough talking. Let me get some music started! I am so happy all of you came to help me celebrate my birthday!"

Mom went into my kitchen and started frying chicken. The music was loud, and everyone was laughing and talking. I took that as an opportunity to pull Greg into my room.

"How can you lie to me like that?" I asked frantically.

"Jay, I was telling you the truth. I found some twisted stuff for real, but your mom called me thirty minutes after I spoke to you. When she called, she was already at your front door with many party decorations and food. How old are you, anyway? I didn't even know today was your birthday."

"I am not surprised; I am used to over-the-top decorations from my mother. As soon as everyone leaves, show me what you got. The suspense is killing me! Oh, and I am twenty-seven, by the way." I answered.

"Ok, well, by the looks of these decorations, I would have thought you were twelve!"

We both laughed, then walked back to the party. When we arrived, I saw my Aunt Tammy admiring my sword that was mounted on the wall. She started moving her hand close to the edge of the sword, not realizing it was very sharp.

"Stop!" I shouted from across the room.

Aunt Tammy slowly stepped back. "Ok, okay. This just looks so outstanding! Can I paint it?"

She was the artist in the family; she could draw and paint anything. I always admired her laid-back, hippy look. Aunt Tammy is the youngest aunt that I have. She is thirty-eight and looks like she's in her late twenties.

"Sorry for yelling at you. I did not want you to get hurt. It is very sharp! But of course, you can paint it."

It was a lot of fun and laughter. I had forgotten what it sounded like hearing myself laugh, and I enjoyed doing it. I am happy I could spend time with my family. During the party, Mom pulled me to the side and told me Thu wanted to come, but something urgent came up. I am sure he only said that because he wanted to avoid the gathering. Thu is different; he does not like to be around many people showing his emotions; he does not enjoy laughing in front of others. It is like he does not want to show people he is happy. I get it because of his past, but he is a different person in front of Mom.

Several hours later, the party ended. I hugged everyone, then fell back on my couch, appreciating the sketch of the sword Auntie made me. She said she will come back to finish it soon. Feeling nice and relaxed, I almost drifted off to sleep until Greg started shaking me.

"Wake up, it's time."

How could I let that slip my mind?

Greg brought me his laptop, then watched me as I went through everything that he found. After five years of working for Child Protective Services, I have witnessed nothing as gruesome as this. I was almost speechless after viewing the content that was presented to me.

"How did you find all of this? Some detectives go undercover to find this type of evidence, but they are not as successful as you." I said while continuing to browse through what he found.

"I have my ways, Jay. Before I went to college for computer science and computer programming, I was familiar with computers. I just got caught up in the streets, then started developing new skills such as hacking. I can figure out anybody's password to any account. You can say that I pride myself on my superpowers. I am most definitely a great hacker; I can hack into your phone without holding your phone, you can say that I am a good con artist." Greg inhaled, then said, "I emptied that bastard's bank account. I did this, months after I recovered, after he shot me in the eye. It was not much in the account, just a couple of hundred dollars, but it felt like millions! It is something about revenge that makes me feel powerful!" Greg chuckled.

"Wait. Go back a little. Is that Ebony?" I asked, fighting back my tears.

"Ebony? You mean that girl who was murdered?" He asked. "I do not know what she looks like, but this clip was a few months ago. So, maybe. But that guy who is abusing her is an adopted kid from one name that you gave me. This is what I wanted to show you. I found all of this from the dark web."

While trying to process everything, Greg showed me a disturbing conversation on a website called *Forbidden Fruit* on the dark web:

```
--------------------------------------------------
--------------------------------------------------
------------------------
```

*Alb1noL1onALCM: I am an active serial killer that has never been caught! I am also a crime boss and sex trafficker, ha-ha! These titles mean nothing to me. I am showing the world how dirty I can get. Seduction of the "innocent" is so sweet because it is easy. They are nothing but playthings, and I enjoy their prepubescent screams. My brother and I do not have the same drive. He believes power is in politics and money. Me... fear. Seeing the terror in these little fuckers faces brings me to my "happy place". So yes, brother, let's show the world our dark reign. We are kings, we will conquer.*

*Sdik3voli: My rapacious need for power will never falter. My brother, you think you must break and bend for power. Not my cup of tea. I am a businessperson. True power comes from those who understand man's need for flesh, and well with flesh I can provide. No matter the consumer, you have a need, I can provide it... for the right price, of course. People act like their righteous platitudes will move me toward their monotonous way of existing. No sir, I am above you. I am beyond anything you will be, and you will love me for it.*

*Alb1noL1onALCM: Do not have me remind you of that, my brother.*

# BAST: Dark Genesis

*We share the same demons, but soon we will unite when safe.*

*Sdik3voli: You are right. Thank you for helping me with ET and that Bast girl. Bet she will leave us alone now! I will never make that mistake again, though. I just want to supply them, not touch them. To thank you, I will get you a redhead, your fantasy! Boy or girl?*

*Alb1noL1onALCM: you know I do not care! I am ready to get dirty! Xoxo*

-------------------------------------------------
-------------------------------------------------
-------------------------------

After reading the conversation between the two guys, I became extremely upset. I pushed the laptop off me, got up from the couch, and then began punching the walls.

"Ah! I need to find them! I cannot let them harm another kid!" I screamed.

"Calm down, Jay! Calm down." Greg grabbed my hands and pulled me to the ground.

"Jay, let me finish telling you everything that I found. This may put a smile on your face. You will get your victory, somehow and someway, when this is all over with. It outraged me when I first read this, and I did not sleep until I found out who they were. I did some research. Look at the first name. It says, 'Albino Lion ALCM.' At first, I thought it was an acronym for something, but I took another look... if you look at it backwards, it is: MCLA. I had to do a lot of searching, but I have their names!" Greg handed me a sheet of paper.

Zhang Yan was the real name of AlbinoL1onALCM. Once he moved to Texas from China, his name changed to Jerry McCain. The guy who started MCLA adopted Jerry from an orphanage when he was two years old. He grew up to be a child molester, just like his adopted father, which only means he was being abused himself. Someone ended up killing his adopted father when Jerry was thirteen. Police never found the killer, and MCLA was slowly dying out until now. Jerry started it back up and began recruiting like-minded individuals.

After I read the second name, I dropped the paper to the ground. Sdik3voli is Tom Adams. They are not actually brothers. They started building a relationship over the internet and became close. That is when Jerry recruited Tom to the group. They consistently have open dialogue all over the internet on different websites because they think it is a game, and they can never get caught. At one moment, they discussed Bast, saying that if they ever see her again, they will make sure they kill her. I am not worried about that; I cannot wait to have a challenge.

"Greg, when they say, 'ET', they are referring to Ebony Thomas! They are talking about her like she was nothing! We have all the evidence we need to get them convicted, but this will not be enough for the court; they will dismiss it. I will figure out something. Keep tracking them. Is there a way you can find their IP address?"

"It keeps changing. They know what they are doing, but I know I can get them. They will slip up eventually!"

"I love you, Greg! I do not know what I would do without you. Now let me go to bed. I only have four hours before I must get up for work."

"I love you, too! Oh, and Journey?"

"Yes?" I answered.

"Where the fuck did you learn how to punch like that? Do you see that dent you left in your wall? Damn!" He laughed.

Laughing, I walked away and yelled, "Good night, Greg!"

The following day, I met up with James on time, so we could check the living conditions for nine-year-old Connor Banks. Connor's mom was using heavy drugs while he was in the house, and a friend called the police after she found her unresponsive. Since they released her from the hospital and served a short jail sentence, she had to complete a safety plan, which includes monthly parenting classes, drug testing, and routine checkups. If she fails the safety plan, she will lose custody of Connor.

"So how do I look, James?" I asked while turning around like a model.

Smiling, he said, "You look like you are ready for action, perfect!"

James always says that if we are going to a client's house, we should always dress like we are about to be chased by a dog! That means a t-shirt, jeans, and sneakers. We must be prepared for anything that may happen. James always does things by the book. We cannot park in their driveway, only on the curb, just in case they get angry and block us in. When we are inside the house, we must stand by the door after our walk-through for emergency reasons. He gives this same speech every month.

Once we had gathered all the necessary paperwork, I jumped into James' car. At first, it was quiet, and I felt a little uneasy because I never knew how to act around guys. Especially guys that I am attracted to. I guess you can say that I am kind of innocent, I mean, I am not a virgin, of course, but I only had one sexual encounter voluntarily when I was in college. It was not a great experience at all! I cannot remember if that is because of me or the guy I was with. I just remember doing a lot of squirming and fidgeting on the bed, screaming, of course, due to all the discomfort I had, then him pausing in the middle of everything, saying, 'damn, you really are a virgin?' He seemed very surprised, even though my real first sexual encounter was rape. I wish my first sexual experience was with someone I truly was in love with and not with someone who was only trying to bust a nut. That was all my fault. I thought I was ready, but I wasn't.

"Can we have some music? This is a forty-five-minute drive!" I said while pressing buttons on his radio.

Turning the radio off, James boasted, "Never touch a Black man's radio, Journey. My ride, my vibe. Besides, you have been under a lot of stress lately. Silence will be good for you so you can gather your thoughts."

"Ok, you are right." I sighed.

I lay back and started whistling. I whistled, 'Mary had a Little Lamb' while I moved my head back and forth.

"I like you. You are smart and funny." James said, smiling.

"I like you too!" The way I said it was loud and over the top. "I mean, as a boss. James, you are great!"

Why do I have to be so weird around guys? I made things awkward, and for the rest of the trip, we rode in silence.

We finally made it to Connor's house and knocked on the door. As the door opened, several roaches ran out the door, and a few fell from the top, almost landing on James' arm. Then the awful smell of the house hit us in the face.

"You people again?" said the mom after looking at our badges.

"I apologize, Ms. Banks, but we notified you of the date and time for our appointment. Did you receive the correspondence?" James stated awkwardly.

"I never open my mail, but whatever, come in. You can sit on the couch." She said while pointing at the couch covered with laundry. "Go on, sit!" She picked up a handful of clothes and then threw them on the ground. When she did that, a lot of small roaches scattered from beneath.

"No, thank you. We are just going to do our walk-through, then leave." Said James.

She flopped down on the couch and motioned with her hands to the back of the house as she searched for her remote. "Go right ahead. I will stay here. The Soaps are about to come on." She grunted.

The entire house was filthy and had roaches and gnats everywhere. The tub looked as if it had not been cleaned in months. Roaches were crawling over toothbrushes, and there was a dirty menstrual pad filled with blood on the floor. James was looking like he wanted to vomit. That is when I noticed a roach fall on his shoulder from the ceiling. I gasped, then pointed at his shoulder. He looked, then squeaked like a little girl and flicked it off. We covered our mouths to keep ourselves from laughing so hard.

"Is everything ok?" Ms. Banks yelled from the living room.

"Yes, I accidentally dropped my phone!" I yelled while fighting back my laugh.

We had one more room to check. When we opened it, Connor was in there playing video games.

"Hi, you must be Connor. My name is Journey Anders, and this is James Walker. We work for Child Protective Services. We are here to check on you." I said as we observed his room.

It was clean, extremely clean. His clothes were folded and put away, his bed straightened, and his toys were neatly in the corner of his room.

"Wow! I am impressed, young man! Who taught you how to clean your room like this?" James asked.

Conner continued to play his video games without looking up.

"My friends," Conner answered.

Connor never looked at us. He just continued to play his game like we were not there. Still, James tried speaking                              to                              him. While they were talking, I continued to look around his room when I discovered a picture on the wall next to his bed.

"Connor, where did you get this picture from?" I walked over to him and showed him the picture.

"Why did you take that off my wall? My friend sent it to me!" he said as he snatched it out of my hand.

"Just was curious. I apologize. I thought it looked pretty cool. Let me hang it back up for you." Connor handed the picture back to me, then continued playing the game.

It was a picture of an albino lion. I flipped it over, and it had cartoons on the back. I looked up and saw James looking at me weirdly, so I pinned it back on the wall. Then, I asked Connor a question.

"Connor, you said that your friends taught you how to clean your room. How did they do that? I may need their help at my house."

Pausing his game, he replied, "Ok, I will ask them tonight. We talk about my game every night when I go live."

"So, you saw your friends before?" I asked.

"Not really. They like to wear masks. They are very shy." He laughed.

"Alright, Connor. Thank you for speaking with us. We must go, take care now." James interrupted our conversation and then walked towards the door.

When he exited the room, I turned around and whispered in Connor's ear.

"Did you ever give them your address?"

"Yes, they wanted to send me a gift, the picture!"

When I bent over to speak with Connor, I noticed that his hair was red underneath his cap.

"One more thing, Connor. What are your friends' names?"

"Tom and Jerry, like the cartoon!" He giggled.

# Chapter Six

For all that is secret will eventually be brought into the open, and everything that is concealed will be brought to light and made known to all. Luke 8:17

***Black****: represents mystery, power, & sophistication*

# BAST: Dark Genesis

I left Connor's house anxious. I knew he would be their next victim, and I was the only one who saw it. Like my mother always says, 'There are no coincidences.' It was fate that placed me at Connor's house so that I could save him. I believe this was them using their real names because it catches every child's attention. There's not a kid who doesn't know who Tom and Jerry are. In a crazy-sick way, it was great marketing to grab kids' attention. I knew this was a huge stretch and I could be wrong, but there were no other leads, and I must admit, they were smart; kids like watching cartoons, and they can watch them all day if parents allow them to.

On the drive back from Connor's house, I tried talking James into putting Connor into foster care since their house was extremely filthy, but because of the safety plan, we cannot take him out of the home just yet. We must give Mom a chance to fix the problem. We will go back in one week, but I think it will be too late by then. I must go back to his house every night until I can get him out of that house. I cannot let him end up like Ebony.

Once I arrived home, Greg walked up to me quickly, like he had important news to tell me.

"Is something wrong?" I asked in a concerned way.

Greg took a deep breath before he answered. "They are talking again. The conversation was confusing because they were talking in code, but I think they found a kid. A redhead!"

When he told me the news, I tried to act shocked because it would be better if I didn't let Greg know I was already ahead of him. It's best if he didn't know about Bast just yet. It's too risky. I told him I will be out on a date with James tonight to get my mind off everything. I went into my room, picked my hair out in a full afro, got dressed up in my uniform, then put my trench coat over it. When I stepped out, Greg had a confused look on his face before he opened his mouth to ask me a question.

"Um, Jay? Where are you two going with a trench coat on during the summer?"

Laughing, I said, "We are going to a party with a Black Panther's Party theme, nosey!"

"Ok… um, you mean like the organization from back in the day with Angela Davis and Huey P. Newton? If so, you won. If you are referring to the Marvel movie, you lost." He snickered.

"Ha-ha, don't stay up too late, big head."

"I can't sleep. I must stay on the lookout for this kid. Even though I don't know him, I must give him my all." He declared.

Hugging Greg, I said, "Do not worry, cousin, we will save him!"

I ran to my car as fast as I could. As soon as I got there, I quickly braided two corn rolls down my hair, then drove to Connor's house. It was about nine o'clock when I made it there. I took off my coat, then put my mask on. I quietly ran to the backyard for a chance to see him through his window, but I quickly jumped behind a bush when I saw him speaking with a young girl through his bedroom window. Who is she? I could not get a good look at the girl, so I tried to get closer, without them noticing me, so I could at least hear what they were saying.

"Come on, Connor! Go with me! I thought we were friends!" said the girl.

"We are. I will come next week. I must help my mom clean the house, so she won't get in trouble. It's a big mess."

"You promise you will go with me next week? Please don't stand me up." The girl pleaded.

"I promise!" Connor said while pulling down the window.

The girl took off running down the street. Not sure what that was about, but I stayed for several more hours before I left. Exhausted from scoping out Connor's place with no results, I was happy he was safe.

The rest of the week went by fast. My mind never left Connor. I continued to watch him every night, and I also continued to lie to Greg. Couldn't have him worrying about me every night. I slept late Saturday morning. Greg was still on the computer, and to my surprise, Aunt Tammy was in my living room painting.

"Good morning, Niecy! You must have had a long night because it is one o'clock in the afternoon," she said suspiciously.

I walked over to hug her. "Good morning, Auntie. I just had to finish up with work late."

"You mean you had to finish working with James all night, right?" Greg said while making puking noises.

"Yes! I mean, I was out on a date... just a date!" I gave Greg an evil look.

"Alright, Niecy-pooh, every girl needs to have a hot dog in their bun from time to time!" She said while winking at me.

With laughter and puking noises in the room, I started going through Auntie's art portfolio. There were many pictures of paintings and realistic portraits of people. I turned to the back of the book, and there were many pictures of graffiti on buildings, and many were graffiti with Bast written under them.

"You do graffiti also? What are all these images of ankhs about?" I asked.

"I do it all, baby! Although I only tag after I hear or read that Bast has rescued a child. It's been all over the news that we have a vigilante here in Dallas. She always leaves a picture of an ankh somewhere to show it was her. It's a woman who has been going around protecting our children. Several people have been locked up because of her. They said she made them say, *Bast forced me to confess!* She is powerful and a huge inspiration to us all! But I haven't read anything about her lately. I hope she did not quit because our babies need her!" She stopped painting and then said, "Alright, I am done! Do you like it?"

"I love it, Aunt Tammy! Just be careful because graffiti is illegal!"

"Whew, chile, if you only knew all the illegal things I do." She laughed.

As she gave me the painting, I hugged her again before she left. I did not realize others were so affected by Bast. I did not quit, Aunt Tammy. You will hear from Bast soon!

"Jay, come over here. I finally found something; MCLA is throwing a parade today. It is happening now down the old plaza where Montgomery Ward's used to be!"

"Ok! I am about to get dressed!" I said while putting my bowl of cereal down.

"Um. I am going with you." Greg demanded. "You are mistaken if you think I will allow you to go by yourself!"

Ugh! No Bast today. I guess that will be a good thing since she can't be out during the day.

"Alright, just be on the lookout for anything. I will print pictures of them both. Tom will be easy, but since they have not charged Jerry with anything here, it might be harder for me to find him, but I will try to search the China data. Hopefully, I can somehow get through."

"Oh, I am already ahead of you. While you were talking to Auntie, I was searching for pictures of them. Meet Zhang Yan, better known as Jerry McCain." Greg handed me pictures he printed.

So, that is why his screen name was 'albino lion. He is albino, and I bet he must think he is some type of king of what he is doing. He should not be hard to catch, and I hope I see Tom.

"Hurry and get dressed, Greg. We have animals to catch!" I snarled.

As soon as we were ready to leave, James called. He found out about the parade from a parent. They said their child got a flyer from a stranger, urging her to attend. The parents complained to the police but were told they could do nothing about it because it was legal. James wanted me to attend the parade with him just to monitor everything. He also mentioned that I didn't need to attend, but come if I wanted to. Cops will be there as well.

When we arrived, we saw James waiting for me in the parking lot.

"So, this is James. He is super buff! Good job, Jay!" Greg taunted.

"Please, do not be sarcastic, and please say nothing to James." I pleaded.

"Ok, ok, you are right. We have more important things to talk about right now." He said while opening the car door.

As we walked over to James, he seemed a little uneasy after he noticed Greg.

I awkwardly said, "James, this is my cousin, Greg. Greg, this is my boss, James."

After they embraced with a handshake, we headed to the parade. I made it a point to find time to apologize to James for bringing Greg. He seemed a bit bothered; he told me the parade wasn't work-related, so I assumed bringing Greg would not be a big deal.

Either way, his behavior is showing me he didn't want Greg there.

Many people attended the parade. There were men, women, and children of all ages and ethnicities. As I observed, I wondered how any parent could bring their child to a parade like this. The parade had bands playing, dancers, and decorated cars with banners over them with different sayings and slogans:

*"A L M= ALL LOVE MATTERS"*

*"LOVE IS LOVE NO MATTER THE AGE"*

> *"IF ELVIS CAN DO IT, IF JERRY LEE LEWIS CAN DO IT, AND IF R KELLY CAN DO IT, THEN WE CAN DO IT TOO, LEGALLY!"*

I cannot believe people are supporting this filth! And, what about the parents who brought their children to support this mess? They are supporting adult men taking their children's innocence. This is extremely questionable.

"Guys, I will be right back. I want to ask this parent a question." I said as I walked off.

"Don't go too far!" James yelled.

"She will be alright, bro... Jay is a fighter! I can be hard on her sometimes, but I know she got it." Greg veered off to the crowd with a disgusted look on his face. "This shit is sick!"

There was a crowd next to Greg and James chanting; *'MCLA! MCLA!'* A father had his son on his shoulders, that looked maybe five or six years old. They were celebrating and having fun.

"I don't know how you and Jay deal with this every day," Greg stated as he shook his head. "Thank you for getting her out of the house. She has been stressed lately."

"You mean, as in making her come to work?" James asked.

"Nah man, the black panther party and all the other random things y'all been doing every night."

James looked strangely at Greg. "I do not know what you are talking about, man. Look, here she comes."

As I walked up to the guys, Greg was looking at me oddly. I paid little attention to it and just assumed he did not want me to leave to speak with that parent.

"Hey! I spoke with that parent, and she told me they only came to the parade because it was something fun for her son to do. Everything is free, including the food stands and hayrides. They are really making this kid-friendly, so parents will bring their kids. She didn't even know what MCLA stood for and what they were trying to do!" I backed up and started watching the crowd. "There is something else. Do y'all notice anything?" I asked.

Pointing, James said, "Everybody is happy, except for that crowd over there."

I looked behind me. An enormous crowd was angry, shouting, and protesting! They were screaming and holding signs that read:

*"IF AGE IS JUST A NUMBER, THEN JAIL IS JUST A ROOM!"*

> *"MCLA WE ARE NOT THE SAME!"*

> *"YOU ARE MONSTERS, WE ARE QUEER. GET YOUR BULLSHIT OUT OF HERE!"*

It was the LGBTQ+ community. They are not happy that MCLA is comparing them to what they stand for.

"Can't blame them for being angry. I would be as well. But I am not talking about that. I was referring to the costumes some men are wearing."

"Costumes? I see some men wearing blonde wigs and others wearing white. I see no big deal about that. Let us keep our focus on the kids." James demanded.

I looked over at Greg and saw his expression. He understood why this was a problem. Tom and Jerry are disguising themselves and have all the men put on wigs; they must be here. We walked around for several hours trying to find anything out of place, but couldn't until I noticed a booth that seemed strange.

"Welcome, welcome! Do you have a little one somewhere?" The man behind the booth asked.

"Um, yes! She is at the other booth getting her face painted." I said while grabbing James' hand.

"Be careful and do not let your little one roam around for too long by herself!" he said while slowly handing me a form.

"What is this?" James asked.

"Please fill it out and place it in the bucket. We will randomly pick two winners to win a new car for free and a trip to Disney Land! Everyone here must fill one out before they leave!" He grinned.

"Thank you so much, I will do that!" I assured.

I filled out the form with false information. It asked for my address and how many people lived there. Everything else was about the children: how many kids we have, their hair and eye colors, ages, favorite colors, and their favorite thing to do.

"Excuse me, sir. Why are all the questions about the kids?" I asked.

"Oh, no worries. This is just information needed for other random drawings we are doing all month. We are giving out a lot of gifts! Stay tuned!" He giggled.

I handed him the form, then walked away.

"Are you thinking what I am thinking, James?"

"I am right there with you! This whole thing is a front for what they are really trying to do. Nice quick thinking, especially when you held my hand!" He smiled, then wrapped his arms around me.

"Hold up, can you two stop all that flirting and let me in on what is going on?" Greg exclaimed.

"Whoa, we are not flirting, and this is just a front. They are doing all of this just to pick out kids they want and take them from their homes!" I explained.

"Ok, so if that is true, we should call the cops, right?" Greg asked.

James stepped in front of Greg. "Trust me, not that simple. We need to get evidence before we report this, or they will not believe us." He started looking around. "But it looks like they are ending."

As I looked around, watching different vendors pack their equipment, a man stuck out to me who was maybe 100 yards away. He was acting suspiciously by constantly looking over his shoulder and walking apprehensively around his car. That's when I realized something...

"James! There goes Tom!" I screamed.

I ran as fast as I could, jumping over trash cans and pushing over decorations, but I was too late. Tom took off in a black vehicle. Several minutes later, Greg and James caught up with me, then bent over, breathing hard.

"Jay... how did you? Are you... shh...?" Greg paused, then put his hand over his chest as he gasped for air.

"What he means is, are you sure? Are you sure it was him?" James said after slumping down to the ground.

"I am very sure; my vision has never failed me; I saw Tom take a blonde wig off before he got in the car. Why are both of y'all on the ground? This was not far." I started shaking my head. "Greg, I will be in the car, and James, I will see you Monday at work." I sighed.

I started walking off.

Greg turned to James, "Bro… I told you Jay was a fighter. Did you see her footwork and how she was knocking down those decorations?"

"Yeah… I did, but did you see her jumping over those trash cans? Wow! That woman can jump!" He exclaimed.

They both started laughing while they helped each other up.

It was about twenty minutes later before Greg made it to the car.

"What took you so long?" I asked.

"Sorry, Jay, I had to get something for you," Greg said as he handed me a box.

"Wait, is that…?"

"Yes, it is, cousin. This is the box with all the forms. Your boy, James, started faking a heart attack in front of the creepy guy with the forms. I grabbed it and ran out while he was giving James CPR!" He laughed.

Hysterically laughing, I said, "Greg! CPR? Are you serious?"

"I do not know what he started doing to him. I ran!" Greg exclaimed. "Hold on... is that? There he goes, running to his car, laughing!"

"Don't just sit here, drive!" I yelled.

I must admit today was very intense, but I am happy we took the forms. We came home, and Greg went straight to work searching for clues while I meditated in my room. I just have a feeling something major was about to happen. While stuck in thought, I hear Greg swearing very loudly and even saying a few words I have never heard before. I wonder if Greg found them talking again online.

"Hey, sorry to interrupt your 'woo-sah' moment, but I meant to ask you, where were you really last week, and why did you lie to me about it?" Greg asked after bursting through my door.

"I told you; I was..."

He interrupted.

"Jay. I spoke to James. Where were you? Tell the truth!" He demanded.

"Fine. I was watching a kid that I think Tom and Jerry are trying to get. He has red hair. I just did not want you to worry." I explained.

"Are you joking right now? Do you know how many redheaded Annies there are in the world? And let's just say, you are right. That *is* the kid they are after. What are you going to do, punch and karate kick them? I see all the books about karate in your place, the sword, and the hard workouts you do. Let the police handle it, Jay." He insisted.

Giving him an intense look, I replied, "Let the police handle it? Do you know how many times the police have made things worse for us? They let the perp go even though the evidence is there, the child! Look, I am being careful. If I notice anything odd, I will call the police, alright?"

"Ok. Do you want me to go with you next time you go? I just don't want you to get hurt." Greg asked sincerely.

"No, I need you to stay on the lookout for me over the net and text if something comes up. I will go back tonight. Tomorrow, James and I will head there again in the morning."

"Damn, Jay. You are very persistent! I hope you have the right kid." Greg snapped.

"They sent him a picture of an albino lion; I have the right kid," I added.

"Well, damn. You might be right, or this is one huge coincidence! By the way, they were furious on the net because they lost their forms. They kept saying AJ will fix everything, but who is AJ?" He asked.

"I am not sure, but I'm about to find out!" I promised.

When it was time, I dressed up and headed out. Greg almost questioned my trench coat again, but he decided not to.

As usual, after I made it to Connor's house, I sat in the same spot behind the bush.

I was there for about one hour when I saw that same little girl who was there last week, walking towards Connor's window, but this time the backyard porch light was on. As she stepped closer to the light, I surprisingly recognized her! That is Amber Johnson, a girl I rescued from a guy who was using her as a sex slave. She was short, maybe five feet, but Amber must be seventeen or eighteen by now. She had her hair in pigtails and had on cartoon pajamas, and right now she was jumping up and down and clapping because Connor was climbing out of his bedroom window. 'What are they doing right now, and how does she know Connor?' I watched closely. Amber was talking to Connor, but I could not hear what she was saying. They were walking towards the front of the house. Connor started shaking his head no, then tried to turn around, but Amber pushed him forward and motioned for him to keep walking.

I had had enough. I slowly started moving forward in a way that they would not notice me, but before I could make my presence known, a black car pulled up in front of the house. A man dressed in black jumped out and ran to Connor. They are trying to kidnap him! Immediately, I rushed over, grabbed both of my batons off my back, and jumped high in the air, doing a twist that ended with the baton striking his head.

Uh-oh, I forgot Thu told me not to ever hit anyone on the head, so I won't accidentally kill them. Good thing I did not use all my strength!

He fell to the ground, groaning in pain. I placed my batons behind my back, then threw my fist back, ready to strike the back of his head, when I felt a sharp pain in my neck. I turned around and saw Amber holding a needle in her hand before I passed out.

*Five hours later…*

Slowly opening my eyes, I saw a ceiling fan moving. I was in a little pain in my neck, but it was bearable. I quickly jumped up, ready to fight after I remembered what happened, but I realized I was back in my apartment. How did I get here?

"You are safe. Sit down."

It was Thu, sitting in the corner. Greg was behind me on the computer, looking furious. I looked down and noticed I still had my gear on. The look on my face was obvious that I did not know what to do.

Thu then stood up and gave me a cup of something hot that he had put together, not sure what it was, but it gave me energy, and it seemed like it was pushing out whatever it was they put in my neck. Once he noticed that his concoction was working, he then explained everything to me.

Greg suspected I was up to something since the parade. As soon as we made it home, he somehow put a tracking device on my phone without me knowing. After I left, he searched for Thu's number and called him. Thu told him everything. That is when he called an Uber and located me at Connor's house. He hid on the opposite side of the street, concealing himself in bushes. Greg watched the whole incident unfold with the man dressed in all black and Amber. After I fell to the ground, they snatched Connor and threw him in the car. Greg rushed over, picked me up, placed me in my car, and took me home, all while calling Thu, telling him what had just happened.

I turned around and looked at Greg, then said, "What I do not understand is why you called Thu."

"It's simple. That night, you dipped out when we were at your mom's house, and you stayed with him for several hours. Then, when you finally came back, you did not have a good excuse for why you were with him all night, and I can't see you bumpin' uglies with him. Also, you had batons and a sword in your car. It's obvious you were up to something, but I just was not sure what it was. I mean, the way you moved when you saw Tom at the parade, I for sure assumed you were on crack or something else was up! I just had to find out if he knew anything because I knew your mother, and James did not know. By the way, your boy, Voo, missed out on a few details of the story; after that girl put that needle in your neck, I ran up to her and slapped her so hard that she fell to the ground. I did not want to punch her since she was a girl, but I made sure I made a mark! While I was checking on you, they burnt out! Damn. My cousin is a superhero!" He smiled.

"His name is Thu, not Voo. And if I were a superhero, Connor would be safe. Thank you for carrying me home. You are the actual hero. I live on the second floor, and I know I am heavy!" I walked over to Greg and hugged him.

"You damn right, you are very heavy!" He laughed. "How much do you weigh, 250 pounds. Geesh!"

"Never ask a woman how much she weighs, just know that it's all muscle over here. No fat!" I chuckled.

"This is no time for laughter. We have work to do. Let us bring Con-nor home!" Thu demanded.

We worked all through the afternoon. Greg was on the computer, and Thu was coming up with a plan for what we were going to do after we found out where they were located. In between that, we trained in my kitchen. I noticed Greg peeking over a few times while we trained, each time he had a huge smile on his face.

"Hey! This is it! These jokers finally slipped up! I know where they are!" Greg yelled.

# Chapter Seven

Greater love has no one than this: to lay down
one's life for one's friends. John 15:13

*Orange:* represents harmony, emotional
balance, & intuition

Conversation between Tom and Jerry on Forbidden Fruit:

---

**Alb1noL1onALCM:** *Thank you, my brother, for my wonderful gift! This will be my first ginger, my first redhead! Now the world can see that we do whatever we want! We get everything we want. I feel unstoppable!*

**Sdik3voli:** *Yes, brother! But I was a little nervous at first. That Bast girl hit me hard, I thought I was dying... how did she know what our plan was? How did she know about my gift to you? This is the second time she has attacked me. If I see her again, I will kill her!*

**Alb1noL1onALCM:** *Brother, let me handle the killing, you are the innocent one. I am the wicked one! Her death will be my gift to you! If I come across her again, I will make sure it's the last time! Now, let me stop all that crying in the background, you know I like to play with my food before I eat it!*

# BAST: Dark Genesis

*Sdik3voli: Hold on, hold on, before you do, I promise AJ ice cream and a new game that she claims more kids get on. This is her gift for her help with the redhead! That Bast girl did not see it coming!*

---

James called right before we left, saying that the police informed him that Connor's mom went to his room and found him missing. Police and volunteers were searching for him now in their neighborhood. She told police he had a friend in the neighborhood that he always talked about, but never said who she was. All she knew was that his friend was a girl.

I failed Amber. Sometimes, after a molester takes away a child's innocence, that child can grow up and become a molester also. I was supposed to monitor her, mentor her, and make sure she received therapy after I rescued her, but I got so caught up handling both responsibilities of Journey and Bast, that eventually, I could not handle both. I am not sure how, but Amber Johnson became 'AJ' to Tom and Jerry. She is helping them coerce younger children to leave with her, so Tom and Jerry can have them.

All of this was on my mind while we were driving. Greg found out that the coordinates place Tom and Jerry at a local motel thirty minutes from my apartment. The plan was that Thu would knock on the motel door pretending that he was lost and needed directions to a nearby gas station while Greg would be on the lookout on top of the building next to the motel, and of course, I would try to find a way inside from the back.

"Are you ready, Greg? I know this may seem like a lot for you, but remember, all you need to do is keep watch for us and communicate on the earpiece I gave you. If you see anything, just let us know." I instructed.

"I got it, Jay. With these bad binoculars you gave me, I think I can watch ants crawl fifty feet away!" Greg exclaimed.

"Bad? How can binoculars be bad?" Thu asked.

Greg smiled at Thu's question, "Sorry… I meant to say; they just look extremely nice."

He turned around to look at me.

"Jay, I am thrilled to help capture these scum bags. I will never say out loud the things I saw over the black web…it's extremely disturbing. I just don't understand how someone can think twisted thoughts about young kids. This is all bad! Alright, this looks like this, maybe it, here is the place straight ahead. I will stop right here." Greg stated as he parked the car.

Greg parked the car a block away from the motel. I made sure I was fully equipped with all my gear before I put my hood and mask on. Thu had on a tan gardener hat, blue button-up t-shirt, jeans, and biker boots. While Greg had on an all-black beanie hat, black sweater, and black sweatpants. I looked down at his shoes, then looked at his face.

"What? I can't be flying? They are all black. What is wrong with wearing Jay's?" He questioned.

"You are wearing nice sneakers for such a serious occasion. Only you, Greg. Anyways, are y'all ready for battle?" I asked.

"Yes! But do y'all realize both guys are communicating with each other over the internet, in the same room?" Greg asked.

Thu got out of the car, then walked over to Greg, and then replied, "They think everything is funny. They believe they are invisible, and no one will touch them. It is a game for them, and they do not care who they hurt. The more people react and watch, the more it fuels them to do more harm. Now, get into position. Let's get Connor before it is too late!"

As if someone had just shot a bullet in the air, I sped off down the street while Greg hurried down behind me. Once he made it to his assigned spot, he climbed the ladder, then lay low and just watched. Thu was casually walking with his hands in his pocket, whistling. He continued until he made it to the motel room where Connor was.

Thu started knocking hard on the hotel door, screaming,

"Nǐ hǎo! Nǐ hǎo!"

The door quickly opened.

"Excuse me? Why are you banging on my door?" Jerry asked furiously.

"Wǒ de chē huàile," Thu continued.

"Wait, wait! Your car broke down? Do you need help? And where are you from? Your accent is very sharp!" Jerry exclaimed.

"Duoyishu, tiny town," Thu answered.

After Thu disclosed where he was from, they began talking like they were old buddies who had just got reunited. While Thu was distracting Jerry, I noticed a window in the back was cracked open. I slowly eased my way in.

"Guys, I'm in!" I whispered as I spoke through the earpiece.

"Jay, try to find somewhere to hide. I see the girl I slapped! She is walking with a man towards the hotel... I think that's Tom! Hide or get out!" Greg announced.

"Ten-four," I replied as I searched through the hotel room.

I was not worried because I knew Thu would handle it. While I searched, I saw no sign of Connor. The only thing I saw was laptops, trash, and a lot of wires.

"That girl and Tom are going into a different room. I repeat, they are going into a different room with food in their hands. I think they just went into room six." Greg stated.

"Greg, are you sure?" I whispered.

"It's getting dark now, but I am positive," Greg confirmed.

I eased out as quickly as I could without making a sound.

"Thu, I am out and heading to the other room," I said while running.

Once I made it to the next room, I ran around the back to get in. The window was locked, but I could peek in through bent blinds. There he was, naked, terrified, and crying. They tied his arms and legs up, and he had bondage around his mouth. There were rose petals all over the bed and on the floor. His body was sparkling with glitter and baby oil. They were trying to give Jerry a great presentation before he saw it.

I controlled my anger as I watched them eat ice cream and fast food that they brought in. Connor just watched; I could only imagine what he was thinking. I waited for the right time to make my presence known. Then Tom received a call and left. I hurried to the front, then knocked on the door.

"Tom, what did you forget?" Amber asked as she opened the door.

I quickly punched her in the face. When she fell to the ground, I closed the door, locked it, and then put my arms around Amber's throat. I dragged her towards Connor.

"Where are his clothes?" I yelled.

She said nothing, so I squeezed her throat harder. That's when she tried to talk, so I let her go.

"Closet," she whispered.

I picked her up, then kicked her to the closet. She hit the closet door, then fell to the ground.

"Get his clothes and shoes, now!" I demanded.

## Greg's view:

"Guys, Tom is walking towards Jerry. Be careful, Thu." Greg said over the earpiece.

Thinking to himself,

Ok, now what? What is he doing? How do these grown men touch little kids? I just don't understand it; this world is so sick! Just being out here, surrounded by these perverts is making me itchy and annoyed! Man, come on, it is dark now… hurry up and get this kid so we can bounce! If it gets shaky, I might have to jump down there and help! It's time for me to do more around here instead of just being the 'computer guy' and the 'watch guy.' I can do more, I need to do more. But maybe I'm seriously going crazy because I'm talking to myself right now! It's time I made a few moves to get a few things that are needed.

"I don't like this Thu, please let me know if you need my help. I'm younger, faster, and I have a powerful punch. Let's face it, you're old and I'm just not sure if you can handle these guys."

I knew he just heard everything I said. Was he ignoring me?

## Thu's view:

"Well, oh well... who do we have here? This is the reason you are taking so long; you made a friend!" Tom said while observing Thu.

Tom started motioning his hands like he was trying to use sign language. Then spoke loudly, "Ok, ok, um. Are you lost? Can...uh...you speak...uh...any English-e-sha?"

"So sorry for my immature brother, my friend. He was trying to show me something before you arrived. Do you need a ride to a gas station?" Jerry said while placing his hand on Thu's shoulder.

Thu turned, then looked at Tom and said, "Báichī!" Jerry erupted in laughter when he saw the look on Tom's face.

"What does that mean?" Tom asked.

Thu looked Tom directly in his eyes and said, "It only means what you are; idiot."

Tom started rushing towards Thu with anger on his face.

## Bast's view:

"Get up now!" I said, "Get his clothes and his shoes!" Amber slowly started pulling herself up off the floor and opened the closet door. As she gathered his things, I turned around and started untying Connor.

"Ahhhhhhhhh!!!!" Amber yelled.

She came running towards me with a needle in her hand that she got from the closet.

"Thank you for warning me," I shouted.

I kicked my leg backwards and got her in the stomach, knocking the needle out of her hand. As she bent over in pain, I did a spin in the air, ending with a kick to her face.

"Come on, I do not want to hurt you too badly. You are a kid," I said with my foot on her chest as she lay on the ground. I eased up a little as she started talking.

"I am not a kid. I will be nineteen next month, and don't look at me like that. You don't know my story! They saved me from a creep who did horrible things to me for years. He made me this way! After they sent the guy to prison after they saved me, it seemed like all I knew was that life, that life in the darkness. I knew nothing else."

She struggled to talk, so I took my foot off her chest and sat next to her as she continued.

"Being raped and molested constantly as a kid forced me to grow up fast. Some people have poor attitudes and live in fear, or they have trust issues after having childhood trauma like mine. I had all of that plus sex issues. I only felt comfortable doing the things that they taught me, and that is how I came across like-minded individuals. I- I am so sorry, Connor! Please, do not end up like me. I am a monster!"

As she cried, I slowly tied her up using the same rope she used on Connor. I guess she noticed I was being easy on her and took my empathy for weakness. She quickly kneed me in the face when she saw an opportunity to do it, then stood up and ran out the door when I fell over. Mumbling to myself, 'I fucked up.' I was looking at Amber as the victim she once was, instead of the perpetrator. No point in rushing after her, I needed to make sure Connor is out of harm's way.

I rushed to dress Connor, then we hurried out the door. I made sure he stayed close to me.

As soon as we made it out, Greg started yelling in my ear.

"Mayday- Mayday! Thu is in trouble!"

I instantly grabbed Connor's hand and told him to run as fast as he could. As we got closer, I saw Thu fighting with Tom. He was moving so fast that I could not keep up. His feet and hands kept rotating off his face like they were taking turns. Jerry was just standing there watching, but once Tom fell to the ground, I noticed Jerry putting his hands in his pocket, reaching for something.

"Stay right here, Connor!" I made him hide behind a bush. "Don't get up no matter what! I will come back."

I ran as fast as I could while grabbing one baton from behind my back. I yelled, 'Knife!' After I saw it to warn Thu.

Thu quickly jumped back, then I smacked the knife out of Jerry's hand with my baton while grabbing my other baton with my left arm. I did a combination of both batons on his face and mid-body. Thu whistled at me for one baton because Tom was standing up. I threw it in the air for him, then I did a last jump, whacking Jerry several times again in the face with a kick to follow. He fell to the ground, lying next to Tom. Not sure what Thu did to him, but it completely knocked him out.

"I know who you are. I remember you! When you started fighting, your moves looked very familiar to me. You are a murderer; you killed my father!" Jerry screamed as he pointed at Thu.

"Hey! Hey!" I looked up. Greg was waving his hands, screaming. "Twelve, twelve!"

Ignoring Jerry. Thu asked, "Why is Greg saying that?"

"We must go. Cops are coming!" I replied.

As I was getting everything to leave, I looked back to where Connor was. I did not see him.

"Greg, do you see Connor anywhere? I had him hiding behind that bush!" I said, pointing.

Greg searched for him with the binoculars. Looked back at me, then dropped his head.

"Jay, we have to go now!"

We took off running as fast as we could and then met each other in the car.

"Greg! Did you see Connor?" I yelled.

"He's gone. That same girl pushed him into a car that was waiting for them, then took off. I could not see the driver."

How did I let this happen again? I was so close to getting Connor home to his family, and I messed up again. Words could not express the amount of disappointment I had with myself. I knew Connor was frightened; I had to save him as soon as possible!

Several days had passed since the fight with Tom and Jerry. Police arrested them, but they were not talking. I blamed myself for everything. I was too soft on Amber, and now Connor was still missing. People were all over social media, asking where Bast was. They used to give me so much praise before. Now they didn't like me because I couldn't save Connor. Days turned into weeks, then weeks turned quickly into months. Still no leads and no sign of Amber and Connor.

"Get yo musty ass out of the bed and get some work done. Matter of fact, go take a long bath!" Greg demanded. "You can't win them all, Jay. Didn't Aunty ever tell you that failure only happens after you give up? Do you give up?" He asked.

I rose from my bed, rubbing my eyes. "Thank you for interrupting my sleep, Greg, but no, I didn't give up," I replied with low confidence. I'm just trying to come up with a plan.

"Jay, it's noon, and it's Tuesday. Everybody keeps calling. They are worried about you, and so am I." Greg said while opening my blinds. He turned towards me and took a deep breath. "I have something to show you. You're not gonna like it, but you need to be strong."

Just as I suspected, Greg had me turn on the news. It was about Connor. They dumped him in front of his mom's house. He was barely breathing, he was sexually assaulted, and he was severely beaten. To top it off, he had an ankh written on his forehead with his blood.

"Jay, he's in ICU on Riverside, and they released Tom and Jerry from jail yesterday due to lack of evidence. They could not hold them." Greg grunted.

My heart was racing fast, trying to comprehend everything. "Greg, none of this makes any sense; after they released Tom and Jerry from jail, Connor shows up at his mother's house with life-threatening injuries the next day, but he's alive? This isn't a part of their M.O., especially Jerry's. He would never allow a victim to leave his possession like that so quickly and still be alive. Also, they put an ankh on his forehead to get Bast's attention. If Connor survived and talked, that's all the evidence needed to put Tom and Jerry behind bars for good and possibly anybody else who's with MCLA. Remember, someone was waiting for Amber in a car that day she got away with Connor. I must call Thu, I must go to the hospital and check on Connor, I must call James and see if they have cops keeping watch on Connor, did Connor get away by himself? He's only nine! I must..."

"What you need to do is take yo musty ass a bath!" Greg interrupted. "I will make the calls for you, clean yo self up, and I will handle the rest!"

Greg may seem rude, but his intentions are great. I love him and I am glad he's here to help me with this.

# Chapter Eight

Where there is no guidance, the people fail,
but in abundance of counselors there is
victory. Proverbs 11:14

*Yellow:* *represents faith, divine nature &*
*mental stimulation*

After three days of being in the hospital and having multiple surgeries, Connor was showing progress and was out of the ICU. Connor's mother was requesting no visitors for Connor and was standing firm on that request. She was feeling a huge amount of stress and guilt for Connor's abduction. She blamed herself for not being fully aware that he was being targeted.

The following week, I went back to work, trying to get caught up with paperwork. James seemed like he was trying to avoid me and barely made eye contact after speaking to him. Did I make him angry?

"Good morning, James, sorry for interrupting you. Can I talk to you for a sec?" I said while walking in.

James had his entire office smelling like the cologne he was wearing. It's the kind that smells expensive and instantly makes me weak in the knees. His smell plus the attraction I already had for him just made me instantly hot, so hot that I was feeling moist.

"Ms. Anders! I'm feeling like your mother never taught you to knock on doors." James said with a smirk on his face.

"Oh, I'm sorry, I-I didn't mean to intrude. I just wanted to reach out about Connor Banks." I said nervously.

James had a smile on his face as he picked up several books and files that were placed in a chair in front of his desk. I think he was checking me out, or maybe I just wanted him to. "You're fine. I'm messing with you.

Please, come in, close the door, and take a seat." He motioned for me to sit down. "I just got off the phone talking about his case. His mom is beating herself up about everything. If you're not a doctor or nurse, she's not allowing anyone to come into the room."

"Do you blame her? Connor has been through a lot at home, and now he's been abused and sexually assaulted by people who haven't been caught yet! Is there a way we can go to the hospital to talk to him? It would be better if he saw familiar faces. Maybe then he'll feel better about opening, and maybe Ms. Banks would feel better as well." My tone was a little explosive, but I wanted James to know how serious I was.

While grabbing both my hands, James looked me in my eyes and peacefully said, "Calm down. I know how strongly invested you get into every case that comes your way, but you can't allow them to consume you. Bad people do bad things, and we can't save everybody. I will make some calls to see if we can talk to Connor. In the meantime, I need you to inhale, count to four while holding your breath, then exhale while counting to four. Count in your head, do this every time you feel stressed."

We practiced doing it a few times together. The entire time, he never let my hands go, looking directly into my eyes. Each time we practiced I leaned in closer to him, hoping he would kiss me. By the eighth time, I was very close to his lips; it looked as if he was about to lean in for a kiss! I closed my eyes, exhaled, then... my phone rang. James let go of my hands as I opened my eyes. I could see the disappointment on his face. I just sat there.

"Are you going to answer that? Seems important." James asked while clearing his throat.

It was Greg. He's now texting back-to-back, telling me to call him right now.

"I'm sorry, James, it's Greg. Everything is an emergency with him. I'm sure we just ran out of milk or something." I said as I awkwardly laughed.

"No worries, Jour... Ms. Anders, family over everything. Just be sure to use those breathing techniques. Hopefully, they will be useful for you." James stood up and walked to the door. When he opened it for me, I could tell he wanted to say something else, but he didn't.

"Thank you, James, I will!" I replied softly.

Dragging my feet out of his office, I watched James' door close and took it as if that was the ending chapter of our romantic fairy tale.

"Greg," I mumbled.

As soon as I made it into my office, I called Greg with the intention of using every curse word I could think of. Before he told me he found Tom and Jerry on the dark web again, he kept saying that there was a twist! He then sent a picture of the conversation to me:

---------------------------------------------------

-------------------------------------

**Alb1noL1onALCM:** *So much has happened, brother, in just a few weeks. I am relieved they had nothing on us, and I am upset!*

**Sdik3voli***: Calm down, brother. I will get you another redhead soon. We must lie low right now. Everything is getting messy!*

**Alb1noL1onALCM:** *No! I want him back!! What happened? How did he get away?? Nothing makes sense! I wasn't done playing with him yet! ='(*

**Sdik3voli***: I don't understand it either, brother. AJ said she dozed off to sleep while we were in the shower. When we got up, he was gone.*

**Alb1noL1onALCM:** *I just don't understand, is someone trying to punish me? All I do is offer love to deserving kids. Ginger was the only thing that kept a smile on my face since that Bast girl and Long Quan ruined everything!!*

*Torturing and killing them will be my greatest accomplishment! 8D*

***Sdik3voli****: So, you say that I do not make you smile? I give you so many gifts, all the trouble I went through just to get you the redhead... do you mean I didn't even make you smile when we were in the shower together? :/*

***Alb1noL1onALCM****: Now calm down, brother. I forget how soft you are. Come to my room and let's put a plan together to get my friend back. We may need to ask for favors to help get him. Ugh! They say it takes a village... the kids these days are so rebellious! He will learn the rules after we get him back! >_<*

***Sdik3voli****: I hate when you call me soft, but ok. XOXO*

------------------------------------------------

-------------------------------------

After reading the text, James walked into my office and said, "Jump in my car. We have the green light to speak to Connor."

The ride in the car was quiet, but this time it felt a little awkward. I wanted to let James know how I felt about him, but it's never the right time to do it. I couldn't get out of my head that Connor barely survived and could escape. Connor couldn't walk with those types of injuries, but what's even more alarming was Jerry asking other MCLA members for help. It could be anybody involved now. I had to keep my eyes open!

"What's on your mind? You seem like you're lost in thought." James said while rubbing my shoulder.

"Ahhh... ahem... I mean, keep your hands on the wheel, sir, we don't need any accidents!" I smiled and placed his arm back on the steering wheel.

"Haha. Ok, ok, I'm trying to look out for you. I know you are worried about Connor. This whole situation is crazy, but with your help, I know Connor will feel safe and hopefully be willing to talk with you. Alright, we are here, it's game time!" James said as he looked for a parking spot.

I sat in silence as I watched him constantly move his car back and forth several times into a parking spot as if he had OCD. James was very meticulous about everything, especially when he was parking his car; if it wasn't perfect, he would keep doing it until it was. 'Ok, Journey, get focused.' I said to myself as we finally parked.

I was already seeing a few cops walking around the perimeter outside of the hospital. This was good.

Hopefully, there were even more around Connor's room. When we walked inside, the clerk gave James a hard time after he said we were there for Connor, so I started walking around to see if I noticed anything odd. Everything seemed to check out so far. Several cops were inside, and they had Connor in a secluded area since he was a special case. Just as I was about to turn around and check on James, I noticed a doctor down the hall who kept looking at me. After noticing him, he immediately looked down at his clipboard and started walking away. I followed him, but then James yelled my name.

Connor's mom was standing next to James. As I got closer, I got a better look at her. She looked horrible. It was obvious she hadn't showered in a while, and she reeked of cigarettes. Regardless, I gave her a heart-to-heart hug.

Staring directly into her eyes, I asked, "How are you holding up, Ms. Banks?"

"Better now that I have my baby back, but I'm devastated that this happened to him! How could they rape my baby? He's only nine years old!"

As she groaned, I grabbed her hands.

"Don't beat yourself up over this, Ms. Banks. With the police's help, we will do everything in our power to find out who did this to Connor. Has he said anything to the police yet?"

While taking a pack of cigarettes out of her purse, Ms. Connor paused, then replied, "Nope, Connor is not talking to anyone, not even me. I'm afraid you probably wasted your time coming because he's afraid to talk. You know, I may not be a perfect mom, but I did everything by myself. His daddy was never there for him. He went to prison when Connor was just a few months old, but he got out after a few years and got a great-paying job! He makes more than me; I'm only getting welfare checks and he still doesn't want to help me. I'm tired of always being tired. Why does everybody want to hurt my baby? Why?"

"Ms. Banks, come with me. Let's give you a break and allow Ms. Anders to watch Connor while you get freshened up and eat something. Would you like that?" James asked.

"I guess that's fine." She said.

As they began walking down the hall, I slowly opened the door to Connor's room. Connor was watching cartoons while eating jello.

"Hello, Connor. My name is Ms. Anders. Remember me? I'm here to check on you." At first, he ignored me, but then he turned around and looked at me.

"She said you would come. She said you are nice, and I should trust you," Connor whispered.

"Who told you that?" I asked.

"Her name is AJ. She is my friend. She told me to only talk to you because you helped her a long time ago. I was angry at her at first because she gave me to those guys who hurt me, but she said they went too far and hurt me too bad, so she helped me escape. AJ said I couldn't talk to anyone but you because Tom and Jerry have friends everywhere, and they will take me again!" Connor cried. "Do you think you can keep me safe? I can't go back to them!"

"Connor, I will do everything in my power to protect you. She's right, stay quiet. It's hard to tell who's trustworthy right now, but I will figure something out. Do you know where AJ is right now?"

"Yes, she's…"

"He's talking?" Connor's mom ran in and started hugging and kissing him on his cheeks.

While she was embracing Connor, I walked over to James and whispered. "I need more time alone with Connor. He was just giving me some much-needed information. He won't talk while Mom is in the room."

Just as James was about to speak, a doctor walked into the room. "Excuse me, everyone, sorry to interrupt. I am Dr. Ryker Rodriguez." He shook our hands. "I wasn't aware Connor had visitors. Will you give us a second so I can speak with Mom and Connor?"

"No problem. We will stand out in the hallway," said James.

As James placed his hand on my back to lead me out of the room. My Bast radar stayed on full alert. I didn't make it obvious, but that was the same doctor who was staring at me in the hallway earlier. He seemed a little nervous and never gave me direct eye contact. I was getting bad vibes about this doctor.

We waited for about ten minutes until the doctor came out.

"I apologize. Connor fell asleep on me. I guess reading results were too boring for him!" Dr. Rodriguez chuckled awkwardly. "Please, come back at another time since Mom is lying down as well."

"Wow! That was quick. It's only three in the afternoon. Were the results that bad?" James asked.

"I am not at liberty to discuss private matters with you, but please come back tomorrow." Dr. Rodriguez stated. He stood next to the door like he was guarding it and held his clipboard up against his chest. I just stood there observing him, watching his every move, making him feel uncomfortable. He began to sweat and tap his fingers on the back of the clipboard. I stood there in silence, staring at him. What did you do, Dr. Rodriguez? I know you did something.

"Um… ok, please let them know we will come back tomorrow. Thank you for your time." James said while he tugged on my arm, guiding me out the door. I gave Dr. Rodriguez one last stare-down before I left. He knew I knew something was up.

The ride back to work was different. James kept looking over at me, but he said nothing. After about five minutes, he finally asked me if anything at the hospital seemed strange to me.

"It was strange. Something is going to happen today. I can feel it. We need more cops at the hospital!" I shouted.

"Whoa, calm down, Ms. Anders. I agree. Everything seemed off with that doctor, but I'm sure everything that has happened is in Connor's favor. They are only trying to keep him safe," said James.

"Keep him safe? They are the ones hurting him!" Someone in the back seat shouted.

Without hesitation, I swiftly turned around and punched the intruder in the face. After they bent over in agony, I grabbed their throat and squeezed as hard as I could. Not realizing the entire time, this startled James, and he almost lost control of the car for a second.

"What the fuck! Who is this in my car? You are killing her! Let her go!" James yelled.

I slowly eased my grip, noticing that it was a girl. She placed her hands around her neck, breathing hard. James pulled over on the side of the road.

"It's me, Amber, Amber John- John-son," She gargled.

Pretending that I felt bad for hitting her, I checked her out, making sure there weren't any bruises. "Sorry, I didn't realize it was you."

"Wait a minute, who are you, and how did you get in my car? I know I locked it." James asked, his eyes beaming directly at Amber. "And Journey, where did you learn how to punch like that? You moved so fast; I didn't know whether to scream or rejoice. Damn!"

Trying not to laugh, I faced James. "I'm sorry. I react differently when I'm frightened. She startled me. I didn't know what to do, and do you remember Amber? She was a client of mine that I had several years ago."

Amber took a deep breath before she spoke. "Listen, I'm sorry for breaking into your car. I learned a few tricks while being on the streets, but that's not important. We need to go back to the hospital. Connor is in danger! I saw you when you arrived at the hospital. I knew you would be in and out. All eyes are on him. You can't trust anyone, not even cops. I tried to get Bast involved, that's why I placed an ankh symbol on Connor's face, but that maniac never showed up."

Interrupting her, I yelled, "Wait! Why the sudden interest in Connor's safety? Weren't you the one who placed Connor in this situation in the first place? You are part of the reason he's hurt. He trusted you and you betrayed him!"

"Ok, ok, let's calm down, everyone... that's a huge accusation to make, Journey. What makes you think

Amber had anything to do with that? She's only trying to help him." James retorted.

"No, she's right. I am not sure how she knows, but she is right. They tell me to do everything, you know, their dirty work, but I am tired of doing it. I'm ready to tell it all. They promised me they wouldn't hurt him too badly, but they almost killed him! I'm done hurting people. I don't want to have anything to do with it anymore! We must hurry and go back before Ryker sees him," she demanded.

After Amber finished talking, James asked a lot of questions. He wanted to make sure Amber knew what she was talking about. He had a hard time believing that there were police officers involved with MCLA. I believed her at the very beginning, but I couldn't trust her. She fooled me once. I will make sure that it won't happen again.

Cutting off their conversation, I asked, "Hold on, Amber, did you say we have to hurry before Ryker sees him? That's the doctor, right?"

"Yes, he is one of Tom and Jerry's many accomplices. There are people all around who follow them. They worship them, Jerry especially. They treat him like he's a god, and they would do anything for him." She replied.

Surprised, James placed his hands over his mouth and said, "Whoa, he just had us leave. Said that Connor and his mom went to sleep."

"No! We must go back now! I think that doctor drugged them. Everything is happening right now!" Cried, Amber.

At this point, I have no time to get involved with Bast. I will have to save Connor as myself, Journey Anders, the social worker, but as carefully as I can without revealing my secret identity. I'm happy James is on board with the plan to go back. He keeps telling me to stay close by his side when we make it there so he can protect me. He just doesn't know that I want him to stay close to my side while *I* protect him.

Even though I feel confident everything will work in our favor, I still secretly texted Thu and Greg to let them know what was happening. There was no room for mistakes. I needed all the help I could get to save Connor. When we arrived at the hospital, Amber went in on a different side while James and I walked in together in the area where Connor was located. The plan was, we were going back because I left my cell phone in Connor's room. The clerk was giving James a hard time again, so I snuck off to Connor's room when no one was looking. I opened the door slowly and discovered Connor still in his bed but shaking under the blanket. I looked over to my right and saw his mom there, passed out.

"Connor, it's okay. I'm back." I whispered.

He flopped the blanket back with excitement and relief. "Ms. Anders!" He began hugging me. "I thought you were the bad guys. They said they were taking me back to Jerry today... I can't go back!"

As he began crying, I placed my hand over his mouth. "We must be silent. I'm going to get you and your mom out of here." I murmured.

Connor whispered, "The doctor put a needle in her arm, and she has been sleeping all this time. I keep calling her, but she's not waking up! He said if I screamed, he would do the same thing to me. I'm scared."

I instantly went over to her and checked for a pulse. She was alive. Dr. Rodriguez only gave her something to knock her out, maybe get rid of her after they take Conner.

"Listen to me carefully, Connor, you have to do everything that I tell you so we can get you and your mom out safely, ok?"

"Yes, ma'am," Connor replied.

"Let's get you dressed. How do you feel? Do you think you can walk?" I asked.

"I feel fine, just sore, but I can walk," Connor said while putting on his clothes.

Just as Connor was putting on his shirt, someone started twisting the doorknob. When the door opened, Connor jumped back into the bed and threw the blanket over his face.

It was James.

"Why are you standing like that, Journey? I'm getting Wonder Woman vibes from you." James said, laughing, but quickly changed his tone. "Look, we must hurry and get out of here. She said if I'm not out in five minutes, she'll call security."

I told him Ms. Banks was drugged. I wasn't sure how we were going to get Connor and his mom out with no one seeing us.

That's when the fire alarm went off.

"James, that's probably Amber helping us."

"Great! Grab Connor, I can carry Mom, let's go, stay behind me!" James said while thrusting Mom over his shoulder.

Dang, he did that with ease! Focus Journey, there's no room for mistakes!

We rushed out the door. So far, no one has seen us. Everyone was running around like they had never had a fire drill before. I told Connor not to let go of my hand and to move as fast as he could. We were just about at the elevator when someone yelled Connor's name. I turned around, and it was Ryker.

"Ms. Anders? What are you doing with my patients?" he asked as he placed the clipboard on the counter next to him. He looked like he was about to do something.

"Oh, no one was in the room with them when the alarm went off, so we are taking them to safety," I said as Connor squeezed my hand harder.

I didn't want to let his hand go and lose him again. Before I could react, two custodians approached us, tapping Ryker's shoulder.

"Hey doc, they need you down the hall. They told us to get you." The man said. "Maybe you should hurry. There's a fire somewhere!"

That voice, it was Greg and Thu! They were disguised as custodians.

"Look, buddy, stay in your lane. I'm sure there's no fire! Go find a corner somewhere and sweep it!" Ryker snorted indignantly.

Just as Ryker beamed his eyes back on Conner, Greg punched him in the jaw. Ryker then tilted his head as if he had some tricks up his sleeve. That's when Thu did a triple combination with a broomstick to Ryker's face. When he fell to the ground, James yelled for us to go. When the elevator doors opened, the clerk who always gave James a hard time squeezed my arm deeply with her nails.

"Hey! I cannot allow you to take him. Let him go, now!" she demanded.

I shrugged my shoulder up and then landed multiple punches to her face, with the last punch forcing her to stumble back and fall to the ground, covered in blood.

We walked on the elevator in silence, with me never letting go of Connor's hand. James said nothing, just gazed at me.

We ran to the car and saw Amber waiting for us. She jumped with joy when she saw us with Connor and his mom.

As James placed Ms. Banks down next to Connor, Amber asked a question.

"I was hoping it would work out. Did the fire alarm help?"

Starting the engine, James replied, "You were a lot of help, Amber. Thank you for that."

"I'm afraid to say that it's not over, Amber. They will keep coming after Connor. We can get them into protective custody, but how will we know they are truly safe?" I asked.

Amber started digging through her purse, pulled out a flash drive, and then handed it to me. She stated:

"I thought this would come in handy one day. This is a copy of everyone who is connected to MCLA. After I noticed it on Tom's computer, I quickly made a copy. They don't even know that I have it! There are even videos attached to it of Jerry doing… things to different people, well…kids. He loved to record himself every time." Turning her head and looking at Connor. "Even Connor is on there. I'm so sorry, Connor!" She said, wiping her tears. "Tom and Jerry kept treating me like a little kid and kept rewarding me with ice cream and video games after I did things they asked. I will do any and everything to help put them behind bars, even if that means me going to jail because of my involvement."

James and I just stared at the flash drive, then at each other, and smiled. This was gold.

# Chapter Nine

Finally, be strong in the Lord and in the mighty power. Put on the full armor of God, so that you can take your stand against the devil's schemes. Ephesians 6:10-11

***Burgundy:*** *represents sophistication, energy, & intensity*

Several months have passed since we saved Connor from the hospital. Both Connor and his mom were safe in protective custody. It took a lot of convincing, but they finally dropped charges against me by the clerk at the hospital. Turns out, she was only trying to do her job and protect her patient; she wasn't with MCLA. She wasn't even aware that Dr. Rodriguez was dirty. After finding out his true intentions with Connor, the clerk said she understood. I still felt bad for hitting her like that. I sent her a gift basket to her job the next day. Greg won't stop bringing up the punch that he gave Dr. Rodriguez. He claimed we could only get Conner out because of his quick thinking and quick punch. I guess he's right, but then again, if I remember correctly, after he punched Dr. Rodriguez, he didn't seem to be fazed at all, and it looked like the doctor was about to do some damage to Greg, until Thu intervened and knocked him out. Regardless, I won't ever tell him that. I'll let him enjoy his moment. James swears one custodian looked like Greg and couldn't figure out why they were so eager to get Dr. Ryker's attention, but he's happy because that distraction came in handy.

As promised, Amber was testifying against MCLA. The secret flash drive revealed the names of multiple people along with their criminal activities. They were in multiple states and were arrested. Among the group, there were doctors, teachers, lawyers, cops, and even two judges. Everything was moving smoothly until warrants went out for Tom and Jerry; Amber let the authorities know where they were located.

## *During the arrest attempt:*

When the cops arrived, they found them in the backyard barbecuing. They arrested Tom but were having extreme difficulty restraining Jerry.

"Don't come near me! You cannot arrest a god!" Jerry shouted in an obnoxious tone. As the cops walked closer to him with their guns drawn, Jerry took control of the situation by hitting a cop with his elbow to their eyebrow with extreme force. That caused the cop's blood to fall into his eyes, making him lose control of his vision. Jerry then snatched the cop's gun and shot him multiple times. When his lifeless body fell to the ground, he pointed the gun at the remaining officers.

"I am a legend. No one can touch me! I will come back for you, brother!" He yelled while running inside his house.

After he was out of sight of the cops, Jerry was even more his supercilious self, as he thought he was untouchable. The smile he had on his face soon disappeared after he opened the door. He then dropped to his knees after hearing, *This is the police, put your hands up!* Jerry didn't realize backup was called after he murdered that cop. They surrounded the house with police officers with their guns drawn at him as soon as he opened his front door. Without fighting or resisting arrest, they arrested and placed Jerry in a police car, where he remained quiet but held a blank stare on his face. Tom was in a vehicle that was ahead of Jerry's. As they traveled to the police station, both vehicles had two police officers in them. Sitting in silence, the car with Tom started moving erratically on the road, then veered off into a small ditch. The cops in the car with Jerry pulled over behind them before they could get out to assist. One cop in the crashed vehicle jumped out, waving his hands.

"No worries, everything is under control!" He shouted. "The suspect tried to take control of the car, and we had to shoot him. He's deceased."

One cop that's in the car with Jerry opened his door, then asked, "How is that even possible with handcuffs on?"

Jerry smiled when he heard two gunshots; the standing officer fatally shot everybody in the car, except for Jerry.

"I was getting worried, Officer Lock. Please take these handcuffs off me and tell my brother to come over here with me." Jerry chimed.

After the handcuffs were taken off, Jerry started beating Officer Lock until he fell to the ground, pleading for him to show some mercy. Laughing uncontrollably, he climbed on top of the police car and shouted:

"We can't make it obvious you are working with us, my friend. We must make this as believable as possible, just in case you are needed again. Brother, come get a few more punches in, but don't overdo it. We are kings!"

Tom and Jerry drove off together in the middle of the night in a car that was hiding in a bush nearby. They planned everything just in case something like this happened. They laughed as they drove away while Officer Lock stayed behind, cleaning up the scene and making it look like Tom and Jerry killed the other officers.

## *Meanwhile...*

"Good morning, Ms. Journey. How is your day going so far?" James grinned.

"Oh, I see you have jokes now. You just walked right into my office without knocking." I chuckled. "I could've been in a very important meeting."

"Well, you're rubbing off on me, plus, I'm the boss. I get to do whatever I want." James murmured.

It was something different about him today, how he was talking, smiling, and joking around. It's just something different about him and how he was around me ever since we saved Connor.

"Well, Mr. Boss-man, could you hand me those paperclips behind you so I could file these documents?" I whispered.

With a smile on his face, he handed me the clips, then watched me as I put documents into a filing folder.

"Listen, Journey," James stated as he sat on top of my desk. "I was wondering, are you free Saturday night?"

"Yes, sure. Is there another case that's requiring an immediate home visit?" I asked.

"Well, no... I wanted to take you out on a date, get dinner. If that's ok?"

This was the first time I saw James this way. He seemed a little nervous. Before I could give him an answer, James' phone rang.

"Sorry, I have to take this," James stated in a low tone. "Hopefully, when I come back, you'll have an answer for me."

As James walked out, I couldn't help but have a huge smile on my face. My assumption was right; James was feeling me! Just as I was about to sit down, Greg texted me and said to turn on the news immediately. I ran to the lounge area where a television was located, turned it on to the news, and could not believe my eyes! Tom and Jerry escaped and killed several officers during their departure. "Unbelievable!" I shouted. As tears ran down my face from anger and frustration, I felt arms wrapped around me. The smell of his cologne let me know it was James. "I just got the news; they will catch them; they won't get away!" Assured James.

When I got home, Greg was so busy online that he didn't hear me come in. I placed my hand on his back to let him know I was there. He then jumped up as if I was about to attack him.

"Shit, Jay! I told you not to ever get behind a man who has been to prison. Greg exclaimed, "I could have messed you up." I erupted in laughter. "Wait, you could have messed me up? Boy, you can't even beat me at arm wrestling!" "Alright, don't press your luck, Jay. You only fight perverted old people." He smirked.

After we both laughed, we sat down and started digging through the case. We couldn't figure out why all the cops were murdered that night, except for one. Why was that cop left alive? He was injured but still alive. Greg searched online to find anything on Officer Lock. Several days passed, and I still didn't have any luck with the case. We started searching through old transcripts that we kept of Tom and Jerry's conversations. There was so much that Thu had to come over to help. That is when we finally found something that has been in our face the entire time:

# BAST: Dark Genesis

---

*Sdik3voli: I am so happy that you have a lot of friends, Brother. Whenever things get messy, your friends are there to help us.*

*Alb1noL1onALCM: To think, I normally dislike locks, but this one comes in handy to unlock secret pathways!*

*Sdik3voli: Brother, I forgot how corny you can be sometimes haha, but I understand what you mean. Without THE lock, we probably would not get away with anything lol*

*Alb1noL1onALCM: I knew he was forever my buddy after he found us in the secret dungeon! =)*

*Sdik3voli: When will we use it, brother? I know you're ready to play in it.*

*Alb1noL1onALCM: When the time is right, maybe for emergencies only. I just don't know yet.*

---

This conversation happened several months ago. This is proof that Officer Lock is a part of MCLA, but there's no way of proving his involvement without incriminating ourselves. Our main goal right now is to find out where the dungeon was located. Tom and Jerry may be there right now.

"Guys, they are calling it the dungeon, but it may be code for something else. We should consider looking for a cave or a basement. Maybe even something hidden in the woods." Added Thu.

Greg instantly began looking around the room, then stared back at us. Then shouted, "We live in Dallas, Texas! Where the hell do we have basements and caves? Next, you're going to say we have polar bears!"

It was so that even Thu started laughing. "So, what do you suggest it is, my friend Greg?"

"Well, I was about to say before you came up with that bull sh..."

"Hem-hem," I interrupted.

"What I meant to say, Jay and Thu, while I was over here searching, I found something that I believe we should investigate. Did you know there is a club that has been closed for several years now, far east, outside of Dallas? They shut this club down because it was a strip club with secret rooms that had drugs and prostitution. I guess somebody snitched, and they were busted!"

"Okay, but what makes you think that's the spot we're looking for?" I questioned.

"That is a good question, Jay. I'm glad you asked! Someone who was arrested in the MCLA sting purchased this property, but that's not all. Guess who used to be a bouncer at the club. No one other than your boy, Mr. Officer Lock! What makes me even more positive that this is the right spot is the title of the club."

"Well, what's the name, MCLA?" I asked.

"Slap yo self, Jay. I know they're dumb, but they are not that stupid. The name of the club is…

Wait for it….

Drum roll, please…"

"Greg!" I shouted angrily.

"Ok, ok… geesh, tough crowd. The name of the club is The Dungeon!"

Thu walked over to shake Greg's hand and said, "That makes sense. They were not expecting anyone to have access to conversations that were made several months ago. Way to go, my friend Greg."

We stood in disbelief after the news. They basically handed themselves to us. We have everything we need to connect Officer Lock with MCLA. We must be careful when we plan the attack. There is no room for error this time.

The weekend went by quickly after all the planning we were doing. We know we must move fast, but we must be careful and not make any mistakes. As soon as I made it to work on Monday, I rushed into James' office to ask him a question.

"Good morning, James. Have you heard anything about Connor and his mom?"

"Ms. Anders, you have to stop busting through my door like this. It's very unprofessional." He grumbled.

"Oh, I'm sorry. I just wanted to make sure they were okay after they heard the news about Tom and Jerry's escape." I replied softly.

"I will let you know if I hear anything. Please close my door on your way out." He responded.

'That was a first. Why does he have such a poor attitude towards me? What did I do wrong? Just last week he asked me out on a date and now… omg! He asked me out on a date, and I never responded! Maybe I should just leave everything where it is for now. I have no room for distractions, but I hope James can forgive me eventually.' Just as I got settled into my office, I heard knocking on my door.

"I'm here, come in!" It was James. He walked in, looking very gloomy.

"Ms. Anders, I want to apologize for my behavior a few minutes ago. I don't want to make any excuses, but

I haven't had my morning coffee, and to top it off, my morning has just gotten worse."

"No worries, James, everyone has their moments sometimes. Did something just happen?" James started walking towards me as if he was about to give me bad news. My heart instantly started pounding hard. That's when he delivered the news that angered me deeply to my core. When James left my office, I texted Thu and Greg in all capital letters that everything must happen tonight! A school bus filled with ten second-grade students went missing in East Dallas. They were supposed to be on a field trip to the zoo. Officials at the zoo were saying they did not have any data showing anyone from that school checking in today. The school didn't know there was an issue until they did not return to campus during dismissal. Two teachers went on the field trip with the students and were not answer their cell phones. What made it even more suspicious was that the bus transportation that they normally used did not have any documentation on that school requesting bus services for a field trip that day, but they left on a bus. The police were stuck on where the bus came from and who was driving the bus. This smells like the works of MCLA: there were thousands of people involved with them, possibly even millions. That bus probably came from another state. By the time they reviewed all the video footage that they had, it may have been too late! This happened in East Dallas, the same area where

The Dungeon is located. It made me believe Tom and Jerry were behind this.

It's time to get suited up!

James agreed to allow me to leave early. He knew the excuse I gave him was trash, but he felt guilty about how he spoke to me earlier, so he approved it. Either way, I was eager to make it home and gear up, every second counted! Just as I was there, I received a phone call from my mom.

"Well, hello, Mother Dear. You are calling me right now. I am surprised. I'm usually at work." I answered.

"Though you walked through the valley of the shadow of death, fear no evil! The Father will never leave you nor forsake you!" She said with poise.

"Hi Mom, were you just reading your Bible? Is everything okay?"

"Well, Thu just left my house and told me he was about to meet with you somewhere, but he didn't go into details about what was going on, and I'm not sure that I want to know. He said he was going to protect you no matter what, and I believe him. Whatever is going on, promise me you are keeping God first!"

"Yes, ma'am. Always!"

"Well, alright then. This is a beautiful thing. Oh, before you hang up... if y'all do that karate stuff, please be careful with Thu. He's older now. I know he's struggling to keep up with you. Just early this morning,

I caught him in the backyard practicing that karate with his slippers on."

"Wait, Mom! Sorry to interrupt you, but why was he at your house early in the morning with his slippers?"

"Alright, baby girl, let me get back to my reading. You be safe now, bye!"

With the sound of the dial tone in my ear, all I could do was shake my head and laugh. I love my mom. No matter what is going on in my life, she's going to make sure that I am keeping God first!

When I made it home, Greg was already dressed for battle with his black sweatpants and his black hoodie. Of course, he also had his favorite sneakers on, his J's. It took me only fifteen minutes to get dressed. I was extremely eager to get out. The faster we leave, the better chance we'll have at rescuing the students. Thu sent me a text message and said to meet him at a location that was a block away from the club. After I read that, I threw my jacket on, told Greg what was happening, and then we left. I admired how he was prepared and ready, not sure why he had a backpack on or what was in it, but I trusted he knew what he was doing.

It was only supposed to be about twenty minutes to get to the location where we were meeting up with Thu, but Dallas rush hour traffic turned that into forty-five minutes. This made me nervous. It's been several hours since everyone realized the bus was even missing. I could only imagine what was going through all the students' heads. We parked the car at an abandoned warehouse and waited for Thu to show up. Before I could ask Greg, what was in his backpack, he let out a deafening scream that sounded like it came from a ten-year-old girl!

"What? What is it? Why are you screaming?" I shouted.

"First of all, I wasn't screamin' but something just flew past the back of the car. You know I'm working with only one good eye: I'm not wearing this eye patch for fashion. I think it was a panther, or something close to it!" Greg panicked.

"Boy, be serious! Now is not the time for games. It was probably a dog or a…" Before I could finish my sentence, I paused and just smiled. It wasn't a panther or a dog, it was Thu.

"Greg, look straight ahead. There's your panther, his name is Lóng Quán. He was the first person to rescue children from MCLA, and he will end that group forever with our help."

Greg opened the door, got out, then squinted his eye at the man dressed in a mysterious outfit covered from head to toe.

"Wait, Long John is Thu? Well, I feel like I dressed inappropriately; both of y'all have on tight outfits, and here I am with loose sweats on. What are we, the Three

Ninjas? You know the movie with the three boys that came out in the 90s?"

"Ahhh!… what you are speaking right now is not important, and my name is Lóng Quán!" Thu shouted angrily. "Let's jump in with a plan. The one we had before was too weak. There are children in grave danger right now. Across from the club is a popular restaurant. Figure out a way to get to the roof so that you can be our eyes, Greg. I already peeked at the targets. Four men are surrounding the club right now. I will handle them while Bast enters the building. I will follow behind after I finish my task."

Greg interrupted, "FINISH HIM! Sorry, I had to say it, Mortal Kombat is my ish! Please continue with the plan."

"It's just so hard for you to be serious," I mumbled as I took off my jacket and walked over to them.

"Journey, I want your focus to be on the kids. Get them out safely! I will try to look for Tom and Jerry, but Jerry will be my biggest threat. He has hidden pain from the past. I must expect the unexpected." Thu said with sorrow in his eyes.

"You're talking to me as if you are preparing me for your death, Thu. Get away from me with that. We will all walk away from this alive!"

"Look, I apologize for keeping cracking jokes, but this is how I get over my nervousness. I mean, do you blame me? Both of y'all have weapons; Jay has two little sticks, and Long John over here has one huge stick on his back, and here I am with only binoculars! Whatever happens, I know Jay is right. We will walk out of this alive, and everything will work out. I'm just glad I am a part of something like this."

Just when Greg finished talking, Thu walked over to him and handed him three small balls.

"Use these when you see the need for them. These are smoke bombs. They are harmless but useful for distractions. As far as weapons go, you don't need them. You are very strong; you just need one perfect punch to dominate your opponent. Remember this: if you must fight, you need to try your best to remain relaxed when you fight. When you go for the punch, use your hips, then pivot! This will throw your target off. Keep your fist balled as tightly as possible, and make a powerful impact! Oh, before I forget, did you bring the communication devices?" He asked.

"Your words made me feel so manly and strong. I see why Jay goes to you for training, but to answer your question, I brought everything, and I also have this bad boy!" Greg started unzipping his backpack and pulled out a huge device. "This right here is a top-of-the-line drone with a camera, video, GPS connections, and even a speaker on it." Greg had so much sureness in his voice, he kept a smile on his face while he passed out the communication devices. "Alright, let's put this baby to use. I call her Big Bertha!"

Greg turned on the drone and flew it in the club's direction. When it reached the destination, he had it circle around the entire building. Sure enough, there were four guys at the front of the building, then he had Big Bertha go around the back, and that's when we saw a school bus hidden in between trees.

"Bingo! Find a window and try to zoom in!" I yelled.

When Greg zoomed in, we could see the teachers and children tied up in a corner, crying. Tom was pacing back and forth. He seemed very upset. Jerry was close to the women and children, laughing and talking to two other men. He appeared to be celebrating something because he kept throwing his hands up and laughing so hard that he was turning red.

"Let me get a little closer so it can catch the audio. It should still receive good audio, even with the windows down." Greg mumbled. As soon as he got closer, we heard Jerry tell the other guys to gather chairs so they could play musical chairs. The person who wins gets to have a date with him.

As soon as we heard what he said, we looked at each other. We knew that was our signal to go.

# Chapter Ten

What, then, shall we say in
response to these things?
If God is for us, who can be against us?!
Romans 8:31

*Red: represents war, anger, & love*

"The importance of perseverance and excellence comes from martial arts; this is the way of life. Martial Arts is a way to get a sense of justice and respect. It is not about learning how to fight to just beat people up, but more of gaining clarity and purpose for your life." -Thu.

"Alright, everybody…" Greg shouted. "IT'S MORPHIN TIME! You know what the Power Rangers used to say? Ugh, never mind, this is a tough crowd."

Just like that, we took off. Greg casually started walking with his hoodie on. Since he had the drone, he didn't have to go to the roof anymore. I allowed Thu to get ahead of me since he was going to handle the four men at the front of the building. I didn't run until I got a signal from Greg.

*Not even five minutes later…*

"Damnnnnn! Uh, Jay? I think it's your turn. Long John is not playing any games! I think somebody needs to check their pulse after the beating they just received!" Greg snickered.

I picked up the speed.

When I made it to the club, there were three men passed out. Thu was working on the last guy who was begging him to show mercy. The blood that splattered after the strike that he gave him with his staff was evidence that he wasn't playing around with anyone tonight. I slowly walked right into the building, ready for whatever was in store for me, but there was no one in sight. It confused me because the building looked empty, and it was in total darkness. How could that be? Just five minutes ago, this place was crowded with people. The only explanation I could think of is maybe the camera captured everything inside one of the secret rooms.

Just as I heard footsteps behind me, I turned around and saw Officer Lock with a gun pointed at Thu's head. "I can't believe it worked! Jerry is a genius!" He hollered.

"I told you I am a god!" Jerry boasted as he walked around the corner and flicked on the lights. "My plan worked; poor Tom was worried about nothing! Now, sit down with your legs crossed, little Miss. Baset. Criss-cross apple sauce! Haha, I will have a lot of fun with you!"

"Come on, it was an over-the-top plan you made behind my back. I am happy that your plan worked, but I am still very nervous. We are not out of the woods just yet. You were so caught up with catching these two that now everyone is looking for us! What will we do with these kids?" Tom asked nervously.

"Is this a proper question, Brother? What do you mean, 'what will I do with these kids?' Um… I'm about to have ten little monkeys jumping on my bed!" Laughed Jerry.

Jerry started walking towards Thu. The laughter quickly switched to anger. "Before I have fun with my monkeys on my bed, I need to eliminate a white monkey first; the one that killed my father."

Thu stared at Jerry before he spoke, while the gun was still pointed at his head by Officer Lock.

"You are right. He's dead because of me, but I do not regret it. Death was the only option for him, and he was the only death that came from my hands. MCLA started with him; he destroyed so many children, including your childhood. Look at what he turned you into. Look at what you have become. You have never had a chance at a real childhood because he stole that from you! Do you even remember the trauma, the hurt, and the tears that came from the pain you endured from your father? He took your innocence!"

For a second, it seemed like Thu was making sense to Jerry. He seemed like he was lost for words, but then Officer Lock started snickering. "Do you hear this nonsense, Jerry? I did not know him personally, but your father was a king, and he only passed his throne to you. What an idiot! Now, do you want me to shoot him, or do you want to take care of the guy that murdered your father yourself? I'm a little eager to play with the little monkeys in your bed, also!"

Before Jerry could answer, the doors to the club burst open, following a loud clash. Seconds later, smoke filled the entire club.

"Alright, pedophiles, if I hear one more racist comment, I will blow this entire building up!" Greg announced.

Greg was speaking loudly through Big Bertha on the intercom. "Sorry guys, for taking so long, I was getting chased by a dog. That sucka was huge!"

Thu instantly snatched the gun away from Officer Lock, disengaged it, then threw it across the room. He then rapidly grabbed Officer Lock and tossed him to Jerry, knocking them down. As Thu did combinations on them that looked impossible to imitate, I jumped to my feet and ran to Tom. He could not see me because of the smoke, but he knew I was coming. All I heard was whimpering. He must remember the beating I gave him before.

"No, no, please!" He cried, "Do not hurt me. I'm tired of this. I'm tired of everything. Please do not hurt me, just lock me up."

Smiling, I said, "Okay, Tom. Confess everything to the police. If you don't, then I will find you and finish the job." I wrapped him tightly with wires and left as the smoke cleared up.

Speaking in the earpiece, Greg cautioned, "Jay, the kids and teachers are tied up three doors down in the back. There's one other person inside the room, standing in front of the door with them. It looks like he has a knife in his hand."

"Gotcha! On my way, keep watch on Thu." I replied.

# BAST: Dark Genesis

When I approached the door, I took a deep breath, then gave the door a powerful kick. This caused the person standing next to the door to hit his head against the wall in front of him and drop the knife he had in his hand. I stepped in and saw everybody huddled up in the corner with their hands tied together.

"That's her! She came to save us!" They cheered. I motioned for them to stay quiet. We were not safe yet. Just as I turned around, the man grabbed his knife off the ground and rushed over towards me. I did not hesitate. I hopped high on the ceiling fan and kicked him with extreme force in the face. He dropped the knife and placed his hands to his face as he bent over in pain. I took that as an open invitation to drop on his back and beat him on the back of his head multiple times. I did not stop until he collapsed on the ground.

As he fell, a loud, horrendous sound caught my attention, but I must stay focused before I try to figure out what it was. I quickly untied everyone and then tried to tie up the unconscious man in the room before I investigated. I ordered everyone to remain in the room and to keep it closed and barricade it, just in case.

I ran out while speaking into the earpiece.

"Greg! Where is Thu? Was that a gunshot?"

So much ran through my head, Greg was not answering me over the earpiece. What is the point of having these devices if no one is communicating on them? I was having multiple thoughts running through my head and having different versions of how this night might end. I finally made it to the front, where I saw blood everywhere. My heart was pushing out of my chest. The pounding became unbearable after I saw a body slumped over on the floor. It was Greg! Without hesitation, I searched for something to wrap around his stomach to stop the bleeding.

"Omg, Greg! What happened? Why are you in here?"

I could tell by the way his lips shivered; he was in a lot of pain. He was trying to man up and prove that he could handle it.

"Don't worry, Jay, this is nothing but a bee sting." He drawled. "If I can handle a bullet in my eye, I definitely can handle a bullet in my stomach." As he spoke, I tried not to show the fear I was feeling on my face. He was losing too much blood. I must keep him talking!

"I love you, Greg, even in pain, you are such a selfless person."

"Well, I had to think fast! You were handling the perv in the back, and Thu was handling the main perv, but Officer perv was getting up. I rushed in and gave him a power punch in the back of his head. Just when I thought I knocked him out, he pulled out another gun and..."

He paused mid-sentence, and his eyes widened; I knew that meant one thing. Officer Lock must be behind me.

"I won't lose you," I whispered.

I heard a noise to the left side of me, I rapidly grabbed one of my batons from across my back and blindly swung it with all my might as I turned with the motion of my hand. The force was so powerful that it made Officer Lock drop his weapon after the baton struck him. This sucka tried to shoot me in my back. I will make sure he knows how to treat a lady.

I ran over to him, kicking the gun out of the way, and quickly picked up my baton. I stood in a position ready for combat, waiting for Officer Lock to strike first. He approached with a sneer on his face. He thought he could take me down easily, but he was about to learn that he had underestimated me.

"Ladies first?" I asked.

He motioned with his hands to go ahead and make the first move, so I did.

I moved quickly, striking with my batons in a flurry of blows. He tried to dodge and weave, but I was too fast for him. He stumbled back, his face twisted in pain. But he wasn't done yet. He lunged forward, trying to grab me. I was ready for him, though. I sidestepped his attack and delivered a swift kick to his side.

He fell to the ground, gasping for breath. I stood over him, my batons at the ready. I knew I couldn't let my guard down yet.

I could tell that Officer Lock had had enough. I rushed over and leapt into the air with a flying knee into his solar plexus. I punched him so many times in the face that it looked like bees had bitten him. Just as Officer Lock fell to the ground, I quickly tied him up and made sure he could not get out. Before I could rejoice, I faced Greg and noticed he was gasping for air.

"Greg!" I yelled.

## *In Another Room…*

Thu and Jerry have been fighting each other for at least twenty minutes. They both were tired and hurt, but neither would quit.

"All of my life, I dreamt of the moment I would have to avenge my father's death!" Jerry proclaimed angrily after striking Thu in the face.

As they faced each other, the tension in the air was palpable. They both knew that this was going to be a fight to remember. The next move came from Jerry, a swift kick aimed at Thu's head. But Thu was quick to dodge and countered with a punch to the stomach.

"Your father was not a good person, and now you have become him. This ends today!" He warned.

The two continued to exchange blows, each one trying to gain the upper hand. They moved around the room, their movements were fluid and graceful, like a dance.

But this was no dance. Jerry was trying to make this a fight to the death. He managed to land a few solid hits, but Thu was relentless. Like a whirlwind, striking from all angles and never giving Jerry a moment's rest.

Finally, after what seemed like an eternity, Jerry made a fatal mistake. He left himself open for just a split second, and Thu seized the opportunity. With lightning-fast reflexes, he delivered a devastating blow to his temple.

He crumpled to the ground, unconscious.

There was silence as Thu stood over Jerry. He had won, but at what cost? The fight had taken everything out of him, and he was left feeling drained and empty.

But he knew that this was destined to be the end. This was what he had dedicated his life to. Yet, he still felt guilty for ending his father's life many years ago.

As Thu had his back turned away from Jerry, he didn't realize he had gained consciousness, awaiting the perfect opportunity to make a move. When it came, Jerry quickly jumped up and punched Thu in the back of his head, making him bend over in agony.

"My knuckles are scarred and bloodied, but the rage that I feel keeps me going." Jerry gave a sidekick to

Thu's throat, crushing his Adam's apple. As Thu fell to his knees, Jerry spat, "Why are you not fighting me anymore? Do you give up?" He asked.

Thu began holding his throat as he spat up blood. He was in excruciating pain, but slowly placed his hands to his side, awaiting Jerry's next move.

"You are weak! Fight me!" Jerry screamed as he paced back and forth.

"He is not fighting you because he respects how you are feeling. He knows he's the reason for your anger. That's called honor." Amber said as she walked closer to Jerry.

"AJ! My favorite girl. When did you get here? You escaped from those clowns?" he asked with excitement.

She replied, "I've been here watching and waiting for the right time to step out."

"No need to be scared. You are my favorite girl! I know you didn't have a choice. You had to talk to the cops; otherwise, they would have thrown you in jail. How can I be mad at you? Because of your help, I could break thousands of flowers!" Jerry started jumping and screaming in the room so much that it brought him to tears of laughter.

As Amber walked closer to Jerry, she noticed a table full of drugs that Jerry had been using. 'This explains everything.' She thought to herself.

"I hate the person I have become. I hate that I helped mess up the lives of so many little girls and boys. It will forever mess them up behind this. They will need a lifetime of therapy, so they won't be damaged goods like me. It's crazy because I know there will be a percentage of the victims who will grow up and be just like you, and others will be just like me. This is a fucked-up cycle that will continue for several generations." She cried.

"Ugh, girls! So sensitive!" Jerry shouted as he handed her a napkin. "Clean your face! This is life. It happens! If we don't do it, someone else will. It's just a beautiful cycle. Yes, the beginning can be rough, but this is the reason MCLA will be legal soon! When that happens, we won't have to sneak around anymore. Children will fall in love with whoever they want, no matter their age! This is a genius work created by my father. Too bad he's not here to see all the accomplishments that I have made."

Just like that, all of Jerry's anger went back to Thu. He was on his knees awaiting Jerry's next move. At first, Jerry didn't want to hit him anymore because it seemed like Thu stopped fighting, but now the rage was too powerful, and he didn't care anymore.

He began walking towards Thu and screamed, "Lóng Quán, Lóng Quán, Lóng Quánnnnnnnnnnn! Did you know people tell me I am angry because I never grieved my father's death? What do they mean by that, really? I cried plenty of times. I still cry, and this happened when I was a boy. It's okay that you don't want to fight me anymore. I see that you have given up, and that is your choice. I am too powerful for you anyway, so let me help you. Please say hello to my father!"

Just before Jerry did anything, the lights turned off.

"Ahhhh! My eyes, my eyes!" Jerry screamed.

"This ends now!"

Amber threw down the pepper spray she had, then kicked Jerry between his legs. As he shouted in pain, she noticed a lamp on the table next to the drugs. "This will never stop. I must end this now. He knows too many people, and he will get out no matter what!" She mumbled. Amber ran to the table, picked up the lamp, ran back to Jerry, then smashed the lamp on his head.

Jerry fell to the ground, covered with blood. "Ah, what are you doing, my AJ?" He whined.

"I'm tired of hurting people, and I know you won't ever stop." She said as she picked up a piece of glass that had shattered from the lamp. "I hate you, Jerry!"

As Jerry lay on the ground, he tried to sit up and began laughing. His laughter started from a low, menacing growl to a high-pitched, hysterical cackle.

"You dumb girl, do you think you can stop me? I am a god! No one can defeat me. I have too many faithful soldiers. MCLA will live!" He shouted.

"You are probably right, but you, unfortunately, will not!" she shouted as she stabbed Jerry in the head with the glass.

-------------------------------------------------------------------

# Channel 53 News

10 students and 2 teachers were saved by the vigilante they call, Bast. She was not at the scene when the police arrived. However, there were several people wounded, with 2 in ICU and 1 deceased on the scene. There have been 3 arrests made so far.

"Good morning, Journey. Have you heard anything else about your cousin? Is he doing better?" asked James.

"Hey, good morning, James. No, no, nothing yet." I replied. "Well, he made it out of surgery, okay, but there has been nothing else said to me. He still isn't talking."

He placed his hand on my shoulder and then replied, "I know this is a lot on you right now. It sucks! He was literally in the wrong place at the wrong time; I know you said he was trying to go to the restaurant that was across the street from that building when he heard little kids crying! He's an angel. He saved those kids, teachers, and apparently the janitor as well."

"Janitor?" I asked.

"Yes, a guy named Thu Le. I don't think the poor guy knows any English. Police must wait to question him because they were saying at first that Jerry put a lot of damage to his throat, they were concerned about his esophagus. It turns out there's just a little damaged, it's repairable and should have a full recovery, eventually." He answered.

"Okay, that's interesting. Hopefully, he'll have an interpreter just in case it's needed. James, what's going to happen to Amber? She has truly been on my mind."

James smiled, then said, "She's in excellent hands. Because of her testimony, many people are still being placed behind bars, and now the ringleader is dead. She confessed to everything, and now Tom is crying while spilling the beans. They will keep Amber safe while she is in jail. I just wish I could thank Bast, though. We've needed a person like her for a very long time. Now, take off and check on your cousin. I know it's going to be hard to focus with him on your mind."

"Thank you, James, for everything. Maybe we could go get drinks to celebrate one day?" I couldn't believe those words just slipped out of my mouth; did somebody just force me to say that? Okay, who got a voodoo doll on me?

Snapping his fingers, "Earth to Journey, earth to Journey! Where did you just go? I was trying to answer you, but it seemed like you just dozed off!"

"Oh!" Clearing my throat. "I have gotten little sleep lately. What were you saying?" I said awkwardly.

"Yes, let's go to Full Moon at seven, on Saturday. I hear they have amazing salmon there; I know you said that's your favorite dish." He answered.

"Yes, it is! I can't wait."

I jumped in my car; I wanted to rush home and change clothes before heading to the hospital. I drove in silence, smiling from ear to ear. I just couldn't believe everything was turning out right, and on top of everything, I was going out on a date with James! Just as my face was turning red from smiling hard and blushing from thinking about James, I pulled up to my apartment and saw a man knocking on my door and peeking through my window. 'Who is this? Is this another MCLA member? How did they get my address?'

I quietly parked and got out of my car, preparing to knock this person out. I tiptoed up the stairs without making a sound, just as I positioned my fist ready to fight, that person turned around.

"Daddy!?" I shouted. I flew into his arms as I erupted in tears.

Daddy and I sat down in the living room, talking about everything for nearly forty-five minutes. I didn't and won't bring up Bast because I know he wouldn't approve. The thought of me getting hurt again would shatter him. In mid-conversation, I just remembered that I was headed to the hospital.

"Dad! I almost forgot I left work early to change and go to the hospital. You can come with me; I know Greg would be happy to see you."

Wait, Greg, who? He replied.

"Daddd…, Greg, Greg, my cousin. He was shot a few days ago. He had surgery, and they said it went well, but he still hasn't opened his eyes yet. I'm worried, but I'm staying positive that everything will work out fine. Mom has been having everybody fast every day since they shot him, and she literally sends Bible scriptures to everyone in a family group chat every day!" I laughed.

"Ok, ok, um… Journey, I have to tell you something before we visit Greg." He said while taking off his hat.

"You're scaring me. What do you need to tell me?"

"It's time you knew the truth about Greg. I told him the truth when I saw him in jail. I'm surprised he didn't tell you already. Baby girl, Greg is actually your brother."

"Really, Dad. I thought you were going to say something like, Greg was born a girl. You almost got me. You're so silly!" I chuckled.

"Baby girl, I'm serious. His mom, that raised him is not his real mom. His real mom is someone that's no good, someone that is still in the streets, but I am his biological dad."

The way he was looking at me, I knew he wasn't lying to me, but what I couldn't understand was why Greg didn't tell me himself.

"Baby girl, he's the reason your mom and I had a divorce. I cheated on her and got the other woman pregnant. Your mom took it hard; she didn't deserve how I treated her, she was very devoted to me, and I messed things up."

"Wait, did Mom know too? Did she know Greg was your son?" I asked.

Looking down, he answered, "Well…"

Before he could say anything, my phone rang.

"Dad, hold on, this is the hospital. Greg must have opened his eyes!" I said gleefully.

I answered the phone, but then I dropped it not even a minute later. I looked up at Dad.

"Greg is coding! We need to go to the hospital now!"

# TO BE CONTINUED…

## The Dream

Out of suffering have emerged the strongest souls; the most massive characters are seared with scars." —*Khalil Gibran*

***Gold:*** *represents personal purity*

# BAST: Dark Genesis

During a late-night walk on a familiar street, I felt as if I was being led to a certain house on the block and as usual, it was the only house with porch lights on. This house always appeared to be inviting and welcoming, but the feeling inside me was telling me to run, run far, far away. I wanted to run, but my feet kept moving in the direction of the house. Something about this house seemed to have some type of hold on me. I know it has a lot to do with my childhood. Things happened in this house that I would not wish on anyone. 'But wait, I'm over all of that! I have a loving family and friends, and have a great career as a social worker. I love my life. So...' "Why am I here? Why am I at this house?" I whispered.

My heart began beating fast when I touched the knob and twisted it. I wasn't sure what would happen once I stepped inside, but I had the instinct to keep moving. I stepped into the house slowly. It was my house, everything looked the same, but it also looked unusual; instead of the one-story house I was used to, there was a huge staircase that had multiple levels, maybe three or four. It was also extremely bright inside the house, as if someone had connected many unnatural high-voltage light bulbs everywhere in the house.

"What's going on in here? Who remodeled this house, and why is it so bright? Hello, is anybody here?" I shouted.

Just as I walked in and closed the door behind me, I looked over to my right and noticed an older lady sitting in our old rocking chair in the living room. She was rocking and knitting a garment as she watched an old Western show on television. I slowly walked towards her as I heard gunshots and the sound of horses coming from the TV. That's when I covered my mouth after making out her face; it was my granny! Tears instantly fell from my eyes; I was excited and confused at the same time. My grandmother passed away fifteen years ago. Either someone was playing a very convincing prank on me, or maybe I was going crazy!

Not knowing what to do, I just stood there in silence, staring at her beautiful face.

Suddenly, her warm, calming voice seemed to brighten the room even more as she spoke:

"Girl, took you long enough to get here. Ain't you gon' speak?" She chuckled. "You hungry? Got some warm biscuits in the oven if you want some."

Nervously, I asked, "Um Granny, is that really you? Is this real?"

Smiling, she answered, "I am as real as you want me to be. I am here for you! Now, hand me my slippers so I can get up."

She looked like her, sounded like her, but there was something different about her. When she spoke, I had a strong sense of peace that came upon me. It felt like I was floating on air, I just felt pure calmness and wanted to stay in her presence.

I walked over to her and gave her the biggest, tightest hug ever! I missed her so much and couldn't believe I was hugging her.

"You have been doing some amazing things for children all over, and I am extremely proud of you. But girl... I have also noticed that you have not been praying like you used to. When was the last time you read your Bible? I don't want to hear that you don't know what to read, just open it up and start reading!" She scolded.

"Granny, I try reading, but sometimes I just don't understand what I read." I clarified.

"You can take a horse to the water, but you can't make them drink." She mumbled.

"Granny! I really don't understand it all the time, it's confusing!"

She instantly gave me a look where I knew I messed up.

"Don't raise your voice at me, you're never too old to get popped!" she demanded. "You *don't* understand, or you *don't want* to understand the Bible? There are many different translations of the Bible. Find the one that better fits you! Now butter my biscuits for me while I turn this TV off."

I buttered the biscuits, then watched her turn the TV off and smile.

"Ah, silence. You can hear a lot when there's silence. Do you agree? Never mind, don't answer that, you seem confused." She laughed. "Listen, you want a lot of things in life, then you get frustrated after you do not receive them. You forget one main thing: whatever you ask in prayer, you will receive, only if you have faith. You must pray, and then you need to have faith as big as a mustard seed!" She explained.

"Matthew 21:22, my mama tells me that scripture all the time. I know I need to pray more; I just forget when I'm going through the struggle. I guess I try to solve everything on my own; I just don't want to seem like I'm weak. You know?"

"No, you are far from weak; you are one of the strongest people I know. You don't let your past negatively affect you. Instead, you allow it to push you to help others! You must pray more, my dear… Keep praying and be prayerful!"

Giggling, I said, "Oh, Granny, I miss hearing you say that! I promise I will do better, and I will pray more."

"That needs to be a promise you make to yourself, not to me. Now, come over here and listen very closely," she instructed.

Just like in the old days, I sat in front of her with my ankles crossed as I did as a little girl. While I sat in front of her, she began to plait my hair. She explained to me that there are three levels in the house, and I had to get to each level where someone would be waiting for me.

# BAST: Dark Genesis

The only thing I must remember is to just keep going no matter what, and just try to make it to the top. As I embraced her and said OKAY, I gave her the biggest hug that seemed as if it lasted for hours. I just had a feeling that I wasn't going to see her again. As a tear fell from my eye, I kissed her on her rosy cheeks and assured her I wouldn't stop no matter what and that I would make it to the top.

## ~Level One~

As I approached the stairs, I took a deep breath. I was nervous because I didn't know what to expect. When I made it to the first level, I heard a lot of giggling and laughing. I thought maybe someone was having a party. I approached a sofa where the back of it was in front of me with three men sitting on it, playing a video game. When I got closer, I froze. I recognized the voices; they were my cousins who took my innocence when I was a kid, the same cousins that my father murdered. When they realized I was standing behind them, they instantly paused the game and then began whispering.

'There she goes, all grown up.'

'That's lil Jay?'

They all said in unison.

They just kept staring as they whispered, then the oldest out of the three looked me up and down before he started talking, "Little Jay, not so little anymore. How have you been, Cousin?

I took a second before I began speaking, then cleared my throat as if I was about to give a big speech.

Fighting back my tears, I shouted, "How have I been? I've been good, no thanks to you, none of you. Well, I take that back. My life has been great, and it's all because of you, all three of you! If it wasn't for you and what all of you did to me, I would not be the person that I am today, and that's a fact!"

"So, what you are saying is, you should thank us?" One of them mumbled as he high-fived the cousin next to him, laughing.

The oldest cousin smacked him across the head for asking that question. "Listen, speaking for all of us, we are sincerely sorry for all the pain and anguish we have put you through. We are family. What we did to you was unthinkable. We should have protected you that night, but instead, we joined in, and we hurt you."

"Ok, okay, it wasn't all our fault, though." Another cousin yelled. "The homie, Al, gave us LSD for the first time that night, and we were tripping bad. We were teenagers, and we weren't prepared for that mind-altering drug, but it was something about it that we really liked, so we kept taking it! We didn't know what was happening to us, and to be honest, I didn't know what we were doing to you was really happening. We thought we were hallucinating; I mean, I thought I was a cartoon character on one trip, it was kind of cool. I can't speak for anyone else, but I really didn't know what we did was real."

I dropped my head as soon as he finished talking. I couldn't believe he just said that to me.

"All of y'all raped me multiple times for an entire year! This did not happen only once; I was too scared to tell anyone what was happening to me, and for years, I blamed myself! When I think back, I never said stop, and I never said no. I made the excuse that everything that was happening to me happened because I allowed it." I cried.

I felt lighter after I let all of that out. I didn't realize how much I needed to do that. After I expressed myself to my cousins, they seemed to understand. They walked over to me, hugged me, and apologized one by one. I was hesitant for a second until I heard my grandmother in my ear telling me it was okay to let go of my anger.

After I genuinely did, there was a finger snap. I turned to my left, and the stairs lit up brightly, and my cousins vanished. I guess that meant it was time for me to enter the next level.

## ~Level Two~

I began walking up the stairs, a little terrified, yet still had a smile on my face. That experience with my cousins was much needed. I felt lighter as if that was something that had been weighing me down without realizing it. When I made it to the top of the second floor, my mind was still on my cousins. I saw a man sitting down reading the newspaper. He had a cigarette lit in the ashtray next to him, couldn't make out his face because it was blurry, as if it was smeared.

"The Dallas Cowboys still didn't make it to the Super Bowl!?" He yelled.

My heart began pounding fast. I recognized that voice! It was Al. He was a huge fan of the Dallas Cowboys. After he threw the newspaper down out of frustration, his face was clear; it looked the same as the last time I saw him. Even his outfit was the same as my last memory of him. When he saw me, he calmed his face, then had a slight grin before he spoke.

"I've been waiting for you, Journey. We need to talk; we should've had this conversation a long time ago when I was here."

My mouth would not move, I couldn't fix my mouth to say anything! All I could do was stand there in silence and listen to him with tears falling from my eyes.

"Journey, I want to start by saying how proud I am of you. You have conquered a lot in your life. However, I know the trauma from your past has affected you then and now."

He stood up and started walking towards me. I began to tremble as he placed his hands on my shoulders and then looked me directly into my eyes.

"I hurt you, and I'm sorry. Yes, I was on drugs, and I was heavily drunk each time I placed myself on top of you, but that's not an excuse for what I did. I take full responsibility for everything, and I can only hope you will truly forgive me one day."

"I was only eight years old! Even with you being influenced by alcohol and drugs, there still shouldn't have been a desire to touch me. My mom told me when I was about six or seven, you scolded her because you felt weird when I walked around with my nightgown on. When she asked you to explain what you meant, you would not repeat yourself, so she left it alone. She blames herself for not leaving you then!" I stepped back as I got louder and fully expressed myself more.

"You ruined my life! I turn guys off by the way I act around them. I've never had a successful relationship, ever! How can I have a normal life when a man who's supposed to be a positive father figure in my life took away and destroyed my innocence? I don't even know who I really am. Am I the quiet, shy girl who is very lonely and insecure or am I the loud, fun girl that everyone wants to be around? Who am I? Please tell me because I do not know!"

"That felt good to release all that toxic energy, didn't it? I can't say it enough how proud I am of you. You needed to say all of that to me because you hold everything inside, you bite your tongue often, and you never express how you really feel in dark situations that you get into because you don't want to hurt anyone's feelings. You suppress your innermost feelings because you don't want anyone to think that you're weak. Well, I am here to tell you that you are far beyond weak; you're one of the strongest people I know. *I'm sure you've heard that before.*" He winked. "I love you, Journey, please keep fighting, and I don't just mean physically, I mean mentally as well. Keep that head of yours healthy and stop stressing so much! You can't save everybody, and you can't win every battle. I'm sorry for making everything so difficult for you. I'm so very sorry, please forgive me one day, but take your time."

Al had a huge smile on his face; he meant every word he said to me, and I felt relieved. It felt amazing to be able to yell and scream about everything I've always wanted to say to him. I even choked on my tears as I yelled at him, but he understood where I was coming from and knew I needed to express myself the way that I did, and because of that, I'm grateful.

"Al, I can't say that I completely forgive you just yet, but I can say that I will try to wholeheartedly forgive you," I assured.

As I slowly walked up to him and hugged him.

He whispered in my ear, "Thank you."

Once again, I heard a finger snap, and he was gone.

## ~Level Three~

The light was brighter this time, walking up the stairs, almost to the point where it started to affect my eyes. I still felt more vital and happier with everything that was happening to me. I tried thinking of who would be waiting for me on the third level, but I couldn't think of anyone. That's when I saw an older lady staring down at me from the top of the stairs with her arms folded, tapping her foot as if she was impatiently waiting for me. I didn't recognize her at all. She was very pretty, short, petite, and fit. She had long grey micro locks that went past her waist. I've always said I wanted to get that hairstyle one day. She has on this…

"Excuse me, can you move a little faster? We don't have that much time!" She screamed. "I do apologize, though; I'm interrupting your beautiful thoughts about me; I can admit I do look lovely." She said while twirling around.

How did she know I was admiring her? Strange.

"Hi, do I know you? I knew the other people on the other levels, but I am not sure if we have a connection." I asked timidly.

"Ha-ha I do know you and you know me; we are one." She answered.

Looking perplexed, I asked, "I am confused. Are you implying that we are related to each other?"

"Ugh, let me stop playing around, I know how confused I can get sometimes!" She laughed.

At that moment, she walked me in front of a full-sized mirror and stood next to me.

Smiling, she said, "Now... really look at us. I just turned sixty in May."

I looked closely at us, then responded slowly, "My birthday is in May also."

"I know, on the fourteenth just like me. We are the same, we are one." She smiled.

I quickly began asking her a lot of questions that no one else should know, and she answered them without hesitation. I guess it's true, I am talking to the older version of myself!

"Listen, Journey, I know all of this may seem crazy, but I need to put a rush on things because we don't have that much time! You can just call me Big Jay, think of me as your fairy godmother."

She then sat me down and grabbed both my hands.

"Journey, you can't fix everything, and a lot of things won't always end in your favor. You can't win them all. Really understand..." She stopped talking, then grabbed my face and looked directly into my eyes before she began talking again.

"You won't win them all, Journey, and you must understand that! Life happens; we live, learn, and make mistakes, but what's more important: we grow, love, and forgive ourselves. We are extremely stubborn and sometimes... well, *a lot of times* when it's not work-related or a battle that we must solve or fight, we are clueless as to what's going on when the answer is staring us right in the face! Therapy is okay; it's needed more than you know right now. When you start, you will realize that you needed it a long time ago. Fighting helps with our trauma, but God and therapy are key!"

As Big Jay was talking, a tear fell from her eye. She was telling me a lot, but I could tell she wanted to say more. What isn't she telling me?

"Big Jay, if I asked you something, will you honestly give me the answer?" I asked.

"Unfortunately, no. I cannot tell you anything about your future. However, I will say to continue to pay attention to your surroundings and the people who are in your corner. You will soon learn that not everyone has the best intentions for you. Oh, before I forget... stop worrying so much! You are approaching the age where your health will begin to change due to your worrying and because you try to help everyone. You (we) do more than just help people; we take their problems and treat them as our own. That's very generous, but it affects our minds and bodies...you can't help everybody!" She shouted.

"I hear you. I will remember everything that you're telling me, but...you said to look at you as my fairy godmother, so that means I get a wish, right?"

"No, that means I give you valuable information that will follow and guide you for the rest of your life! Oh, forget it, what harm can it do? Girl, let me tell you about James! He…"

*(Snap!) I woke up.*

"No! That was a dream? Do you mean to tell me I was sleeping this entire time? Go back to sleep! She was about to tell me about James!" I screamed.

That was the most detailed, emotional dream I've ever had. I won't ever forget the conversations and experiences in that dream. The main thing I won't forget is when Big Jay cautioned me to be more vigilant with the people in my circle because not everyone has the best intentions for me. I wonder who she was talking about.

Only time will tell. I will be prepared and ready for whatever is in store for me!

# THE END

# First Fight

LATOY P. HOUSTON

Journey at Work

BAST: Dark Genesis

# Greg and Big Bertha